MONEYFULNESS®

MONEYFULNESS®

Learning to
LIVE *with* MONEY

MICHAEL KEET

NEW YORK

LONDON • NASHVILLE • MELBOURNE • VANCOUVER

MONEYFULNESS®
Learning to LIVE *with* MONEY

© 2020 MICHAEL KEET

Published in New York, New York, by Morgan James Publishing. Morgan James is a trademark of Morgan James, LLC. www.MorganJamesPublishing.com

ISBN 978-1-64279-616-2 paperback
ISBN 978-1-64279-617-9 eBook
Library of Congress Control Number: 2019907441

Cover Design by:
Rachel Lopez
www.r2cdesign.com

Interior Design by:
Bonnie Bushman
The Whole Caboodle Graphic Design

Morgan James is a proud partner of Habitat for Humanity Peninsula and Greater Williamsburg. Partners in building since 2006.

Get involved today! Visit
www.MorganJamesBuilds.com

To my wife because she had to listen
to all my stories and doubts and ideas.
And because she wants to set up a
Moneyfulness foundation with me.

When it comes to money, you can't win. If you focus on making it, you're materialistic. If you try to but don't make any, you're a loser. If you make a lot and keep it, you're a miser. If you make it and spend it, you're a spendthrift. If you don't care about making it, you're unambitious. If you make a lot and still have it when you die, you're a fool—for trying to take it with you. The only way to really win with money is to hold it loosely—and be generous with it to accomplish things of value.

—John C. Maxwell

TABLE OF CONTENTS

INTRODUCTION

Money is the biggest cause of stress in America, hands down. For many of us, it can feel like, at the end of our money, there is still a lot of month left to get through. We struggle to get ahead and eagerly look forward to the next promotion, thinking a bigger paycheck will solve all our stress. Meanwhile, living without ever worrying about money feels like a far-off dream.

Yet, people who have more money still worry. Within the top 5% of the richest people on Earth, there are plenty who still have financial stress. Though they may have a significant amount in the bank at the beginning of the month, they worry about maintaining their wealth and making sure their high standard of living can be sustained or even passed down to future generations.

No matter your financial status, one thing is certain: we are all too stressed about money.

Stress appears if you have to do something or if something happens to you that is outside your comfort zone. It can either be a real challenge or an imagined challenge. Regardless if it's real or imagined, it feels like a threat to your well-being, like you are in danger. This feeling flushes your body with hormones to prepare your system to evade or confront danger. According to the American Psychological Association (APA), there are three types of stress: acute, episodic acute and chronic stress.

Acute stress is the kind of stress that can appear any time of the day. Suddenly, it's there. Let's say you have a presentation to give. You enter the room and start the laptop and beamer. Suddenly, you realize you've left your USB stick with the PowerPoint presentation at the office. In half an hour, 50 people will be staring at you. Your heart beats rapidly, your blood pressure rises, you start to sweat, your breath is short and frequent, and your hands and feet get cold. After five terrible minutes, you've found the solution. You call the office and ask them to email the PowerPoint to the host of the meeting He will copy it to his USB stick; the problem is solved. Ten minutes later, the PowerPoint presentation is running. You still have fifteen minutes to prepare yourself. Your acute stress has ended. As you can see, everybody will experience acute stress in their lives, no exception.

If you're frequently experiencing acute stress, if there are so many triggers that cause you acute stress, then normal acute stress turns into episodic acute stress. People living their life in episodic acute stress constantly feel overloaded. They have too many responsibilities, can hardly stay organized, and may experience burnout. People experiencing episodic acute stress may react with hostility or with a sense of dread, seeing only negative outcomes in their future.

Finally, chronic stress is the most harmful stress type. If you're constantly experiencing stress and there's hardly any moment in a day that you're stress free, it can damage your physical health and deteriorate your mental health. When it comes to money, we all experience some moments of acute stress, and maybe even a few periods of episodic acute stress. But if we live every day in a state of chronic financial stress, we will harm our general wellbeing (and likely won't improve our financial situation much, either).

Mindfulness

Mindfulness is a generally known concept today. In short, mindfulness helps you reach a state of inner peace, deal with stress and fears, reduce worrying, and avoid judging others. It teaches us to combat the stressors of our lives and work through them. There are hundreds of books and websites dedicated to the topic of mindfulness, especially as it relates to work and relationships—two huge areas of stress for most of us. In teaching us to be mindful in our careers and relationships, mindfulness experts rely on the seven aiding factors of mindfulness, or the primary pillars of a mindfulness practice.

The Seven Aiding Factors of Mindfulness

For those who are less familiar with mindfulness, Jon Kabat-Zinn, a mindfulness professor at the clinic of the university of Worcester, Massachusetts, USA, and founder of the stress reduction clinic, invented the seven aiding factors of mindfulness. They are:

1. **Not judging**: Don't judge others. Try to observe without judgment. It helps you "see" what goes on inside your head. Be aware of your own prejudice. The trick is to refrain from acting on your prejudice. What happens in your head, stays in your head.
2. **Not striving**: There is no other goal than to be yourself, in any form.
3. **Acceptance:** The willingness to see things as they are. By accepting every moment completely as it is, you will be able to experience life more completely.

4. **Letting go**: You have thoughts, ideas, wishes, opinions, hopes, experiences, etc. These can be pleasant, or unpleasant. Stop resisting and stop struggling to achieve it and let things be as they are.

5. **Beginner's mind**: Let go of all your past and start fresh. Be open to all new things and allow yourself to be surprised.

6. **Patience**: Things happen when the time is right. Don't be frustrated because something doesn't work the way you want it to. Be patient. In time, all pieces will fall into place.

7. **Trust**: Trust yourself and your feelings. Be confident that things will present themselves when the time is right. Rely on yourself and trust yourself.

I can imagine that, based on these seven aiding factors, you might think, "This is very vague and woolly." The aiding factors are, in fact, formulated very generally. Being somewhat vague, they give us a framework to apply to most decisions and challenges we face in a given day. But there's something missing here.

Money: The Missing Element

Money is the main cause of stress in the United States. Yet, within the existing concept of mindfulness there hardly is any focus on money. Since the combination of mindfulness and money did not yet exist, I developed the concept of Moneyfulness to address the issue. Moneyfulness is made up of two distinct parts. First, a foundation of mindfulness is needed to change the way we think about money. Then, we need to learn practical skills for managing our money and changing our behaviors.

Everyone worries about money sometimes in the broadest sense of the word. There is nothing wrong with worrying about your own finances or your financial future once in a while. It becomes a problem if it turns into a weekly habit, or even worse, into a daily habit. It means that contemplation has turned into worrying and stress. Frequently worrying about financial affairs and your financial future contributes nothing to your happiness in life. To the contrary, it detracts from your life. Worrying about money only costs you time and energy. Worrying is done with your brain, which is a problem, because your brain is the part of the body that consumes the most energy—energy that is better spent on other things.

Money stress can even affect your IQ. The average IQ is around 100. Studies have shown that money-related stress can make your IQ drop by more than 10 points.[1] This means that financial stress can cause you to make less thoughtful, and potentially harmful, decisions.

Everyone has a period in their life with too much focus on financial worries. For some of these people, there is light at the end of the tunnel at some point, and the worrying reverts to casual contemplation. For a very large group of people, worrying about money is a weekly or monthly activity.

My administration office gives me insight into the financial data of all my customers, both business and private. My customer Marc has his own company and steadily pays himself his regular compensation halfway every month. This compensation is almost equal to his profit. His partner, Eva, is employed and gets her salary at the end of every month. Marc makes a nice living, and Eva has a great job. To put it bluntly, they are two very average people when it comes to income. Still, they worry about money, or better said, they worry about their lack of money at least twice a month: just before Marc pays himself his compensation and the week before the salary of Eva comes in. At the end of the money, they have a piece of month left. They are unable to make ends meet. They don't handle the money they make properly, and they have not built a buffer that would take away their worries. I was

---

1   https://money.usnews.com/money/blogs/my-money/2013/10/23/study-financial-stress-dramatically-lowers-your-iq

unable to get insight into the exact spending pattern, but it was clear that it exceeded their income. They may have inhibiting convictions, or they are constantly falling for the same pitfalls or are unable to protect each other from those pitfalls. The story of Marc and Eva is not an exception. I have seen many of these stories pass review in my administration office.

If this sounds anything like your situation, I'm here to offer help.

My Story, and Why You will Benefit From This Book.

After a false start with my education and work experience, I quickly made up for lost time, and then some. At the age of 21, I got the label "underprivileged youngster" slapped onto me, because I had no professional training or any relevant work experience. I was never without a job; I accepted various temporary jobs in factories and fulfilled my conscription at the medical troops. Subsequently, I was given the opportunity to study again. From that moment on, everything went smoothly. I got my diplomas and built a career for myself. Things were going so well that, at the age of 30, I was the person ultimately responsible for the finances of a transport company with more than 500 employees. I fulfilled this role at various companies—some bigger, some smaller—for a period of fourteen years. I fulfilled my part in society and automatically got sucked up in the rat race. At times, I had more money than I could spend, and at times, I was short on money. The spending pattern adjusted to the income.

Despite my generous salary, money stress always remained a constant at some level. I had to keep my job; otherwise, I would have financial problems. If you don't pay the mortgage, your house is put up for auction. During the crisis, house prices experienced a 25% drop in the Netherlands where I live, and in the Netherlands, you face personal residual debt when the bank forces you to sell your house. If you sell your house with a loss on your own initiative, the residual debt will haunt you as well. The pressure to keep my job and to keep my income at a steady level was massive.

Still, I started feeling the urge to start my own company. Together with a partner, I started developing an online bookkeeping suite. He provided the programming knowledge, and I provided the financial and business knowledge. After two years of development, the software was ready for release. We both quit our jobs and started our adventure energetically. In addition to the bookkeeping suite, I immediately founded an administration office for other financial services. After 3 years, the administration office was converted into a franchise formula of administration offices. After two years, my partner left the company, and a larger ICT company took over the management and development. For the bookkeeping suite, a crowdfunding campaign was completed successfully. I published my first book, et cetera. For the outside world, things appeared to be going smoothly.

One day, I woke up and I had a strange realization. My company was not doing so well, and the debt had grown too big. But somehow, it caused me little stress. I started wondering how that was possible: no money and no stress. In the top three things people worry about all the time, and that cause people a lot of stress, money has a solid position, in addition to relationship and work. Why did that not apply to me this time? During all the years I worked as an employee, I made significantly more money. I usually had a buffer, as well as financial stress. To give some perspective, my company had a debt of $200,000 to third parties, and I had invested $125,000 of my own money and about $200,000 in work hours. I considered the investment into my company to be my biggest asset. Virtually, all investments were made into the software suite. Banks finance software to a very limited extent. It sounds strange, but something holds no value to a bank if it isn't tangible. The money I had worked so hard for had been invested in the company, and on top of that, the bank had given me a private loan of 40,000 Euro. If you have come up with something and are passionate about it, you hardly every quit while you're ahead.

In summary, I was in big trouble. What was I to do with my company? And how was I to get rid of the private loan of 40,000 with the bank? Somehow, the entire financial situation caused me little stress. I explored how it was possible that my head and gut were so calm through all this. Three years prior to this situation. I attended a number of courses in personal development, in which various elements of mindfulness were addressed. Then it suddenly hit me: *All those personal development courses enabled me to keep my brain calm and to keep my nerves in check, without too much effort or stress.*

I've had periods in my life when I had both money and money stress. Never did I expect to have a period in my life without money and without money stress. Being short of money is not pleasant; it needs to be dealt with, but having financial stress is not necessary. The fact is, worrying costs too much time, which is better spent on solving the money shortage.

While I don't want you to experience any money issues yourself, it is my hope that everyone can approach whatever financial challenges they face with the same sense of calm I felt. The first step to fixing money issues is dealing with the stress they can cause.

The Moneyfulness Methodology

Moneyfulness is about individuals who, one way or the other, want to obtain a different attitude about money. You want to adjust the perception of your own poverty. In addition to your own perception, you want to improve your financial situation.

In the first phase of the Moneyfulness system, I will walk you through the Money Method. In this method, you will get to know yourself, your attitude towards money, your inhibiting convictions about money and how you deal with money. How can you reduce stress and worries about financial affairs? How can you let others be who they are and not judge yourself too harshly? Don't torment yourself with all kinds of useless negative thoughts; give yourself some space. Start working on yourself and put a stop to stress and financial worries. You can't eliminate them entirely, but you can keep them in check.

The second part of Moneyfulness is the practical part. You'll map your own finances. After you have obtained insight into your past, you will use the Bank Management System to get your finances organized. This will give you peace in the financial area and allow you to properly plan your financial future. This has nothing to do with the absolute amount you think you need; any amount will do.

Moneyfulness is a practical approach. There are exercises concerning your convictions about money, and you'll obtain self-insight about your behavioral patterns. You'll use the foundational elements of mindfulness, along with a practical system for getting your finances in order, to set yourself on a new path.

By all means, this system is not about becoming a millionaire. Everything depends on your wishes and your spending pattern. If you live alone in a small apartment, you don't need a lot. I am not talking about your desires for the future but about your current spending pattern. When you live in a big house and have three children who are off at college, things are a little different. Your spending pattern changes with every phase in life, but your attitudes toward money don't have to. Moneyfulness is about setting yourself up to handle whatever life throws your way.

Paying It Forward

Based on a series of experiments, carried out by Kathleen Vohs of the Carlson School of Management and colleagues at the University of Minnesota, I will walk you through psychological and behavioral consequences of merely the suggestion of money. A hint of money or even an unconscious perception of money makes people work harder and act more independently.

A group of people was divided in two. One group was constantly confronted with money in a subtle manner. There was a stack of monopoly money on the table, they had to read sentences with salary and wealth, there were posters on the wall with images of money and the screensaver was filled with money. In the second group, there was no single hint or suggestion of money.

Both groups had to carry out the same tasks. The result showed that those who had been exposed to money asked for less help but were also less eager to offer help. The same group observed a greater physical distance during conversations and spent more time alone than in the other group. They were less willing to donate money than the group who hadn't seen any money-related images.

The conclusion from the study is that money is a strong motivator to do or refrain from doing something and money makes you more asocial.[2] Both ideas are based on the same reason. Money provides a level of independence. Even the *idea* of money can make you feel more independent. Moneyfulness makes you more independent from the big bad world, but it does not imply that we don't all have a role to play in the world.

You are most likely familiar with the feeling of euphoria when you give something to others who need it. Giving affects you. A number of test subjects were given a list of charities by Jorge Moll of the National Institutes of Health. The mere thought of being able to donate was enough to activate the brain. The reward center in the brain produces dopamine, which results in a euphoric feeling. The sense of happiness contributes to a better feeling about yourself. If you feel better about yourself, your self-confidence grows, making you more stable. You are changing yourself. After giving, you feel stronger and more balanced

2   http://nymag.com/news/features/money-brain-2012-7/index3.html

in life, which in the end, will make you see that you are working on yourself. You have become a better person.

For these reasons and many more, 10% of the proceeds from this book and its related courses will be donated to poverty-reduction causes, and I want to hear from you about the organizations you'd like this book to support.

In principle, any charity that fights poverty in the world qualifies for a listing on www.Moneyfulness.me. Moneyfulness contributes to eliminating all forms of poverty as quickly as possible in the most structural way possible. Projects that require money to realize this are just as welcome as educational projects. As soon as the project is posted on the website, it is up to you to motivate everyone to save coins and to assign them to your project.

Moneyfulness has a domino effect. When we change our feelings toward money, we are in a better position than ever to pay it forward and to help others—no matter the amount in our bank accounts.

Chapter 1

THE GOAL IS
POVERTY REDUCTION

Beware of little expenses. A small leak will sink a great ship.
–Benjamin Franklin

P overty is all across the globe—the western world is no exception. When we hear the word "poverty," we tend to imagine small shacks in faraway countries. We think of people who are literally struggling to get by, and even though we may be experiencing financial stress, as long as we can put food on the table each night, we do not consider ourselves to be living in poverty.

Because the word poverty calls to mind such specific images, let's start this chapter with a definition of the word as it will be used here. In this book, we will use a wider definition for the word poverty. When you are struggling to live and have little to no possessions or money, that's poverty as we know it. When you're living paycheck to paycheck and

1

have a lot of debt, that's also poverty, no matter how big or small those paychecks are. And the third kind of poverty concerns the mindset. There exists a large group of people who will never feel like they have enough money or that they might lose the money they do have at any moment. Regardless of the actual size of their bank accounts, they never feel like enough is enough. They have an impoverished mindset.

The goal of Moneyfulness is to eliminate poverty from the world in all its forms. Let's spend some more time understanding each form of poverty and how they can be combatted.

Shortage of Money in the Third World

Having no money in poor countries leads to completely different problems than we experience in the western world. If you have no money in the third world, this has immediate consequences for your health. You may not have access to food or water, the two essential basic needs for survival. There's a good reason why, in Maslow's Pyramid, food and water are at the bottom as the foundation of life itself. Ironically, there is plenty of food and water across the globe; it simply is distributed improperly. In addition to food and water, clothing and a roof over your head are the two basic needs a human has. When you don't have any money to buy food and clean drinking water, you most definitely have no money to pay for clothing and a roof over your head.

According to WHO (World Health Organization), you are "poor" if you have less than $1.25 to spend a day. It is hard to imagine how to live on $1.25 a day. In 1990, 43% of the global population lived in poverty. In 2000, the percentage dropped to 33%, only to drop even further to 21% after 2010. The rapidly declining percentage of people who have to survive on less than $1.25 gives hope to eliminating poverty in the world. However, this daily amount still isn't a lot, which is why funds that aim to eliminate poverty will be needed for quite some time.

Methods to Reduce Poverty in the Third World

There are two ways to reduce poverty. The first way is the most obvious method: donating money. Moneyfulness donates 10% of its turnover to projects that engage in poverty reduction. These have to be projects with a clear and transparent financial design. Projects in which money is being misappropriated are not accepted. The donated money must be spent directly and entirely on a concrete project for poverty reduction. These projects can be all across the globe. For instance, a village in Ghana that needs a water well to provide the village with clean drinking water. Another example is a project to support a food bank in New York. Where poverty exists, projects exist to improve the life of others.

The second method of eliminating poverty across the world is education. In addition to projects that donate money, projects that teach how to better manage money qualify for donations as well. All across the globe, educational projects can be established to better manage finances. The better we are able to manage our personal finances, the better our mindsets regarding finances will be and the happier and more positive our attitudes will be towards life.

Money, but Poverty Nonetheless

Mark, an entrepreneur and one of my customers from the administration office, had a gross income of over $100,000 a year. His wife had a part-time job and made $50,000 a year. These are amounts that would make a lot of people very happy. Mark's income dropped from $175,000 to over a little over $100,000 in the past two years. This automatically meant there was less income every month. They kept living in the same, expensive house, wearing the same designer clothing and having dinner at their favorite five-star restaurant around the corner at least once a week. They went on vacation three times a year, across the globe, and of course, a ski trip was also included. Two years have passed since Mark's drop in income, and they have depleted their savings. There even is an overdraft at the bank and they have credit card debt. When discussing his financial statements and tax return, he wondered out loud how his savings could have evaporated. Mark had not adjusted his spending pattern to his decline in income. Later on in the book, you'll find out what money type Mark is, and why he keeps spending so much money. Mark wasn't the only customer at the administration office who kept up appearances but was hiding a deficit or a pile of debt behind the front door. Having plenty of income but having even more expenses is a common problem in our society.

Methods to Reduce Poverty in the Western World

The first way to reduce poverty in the western world is through education, especially for those who have an income but do not know how to manage it, like Mark. In the current school system, there is little room for financial education, not even in economic studies. In school, the subject of economics is taught, but this hardly includes any knowledge about your personal finances, like how to deal with your own wallet. I have yet to encounter initiatives to teach children how to properly handle their own money at schools, at least not in a structural way like the method used to teach math or languages.

Because very few people have attended the school of personal finances, there are countless adults who do not know how to wisely manage their money. They worry about financial matters, and it gives them stress. Moneyfulness supports projects all across the globe in which education is provided about personal finances in a structural manner. By investing in education concerning your finances, you can help eliminate poverty at a later age. Education is a long-term investment.

The second method is volunteering, either your time or your resources. The food bank is a great example of a charity in the western world. There are a lot of harrowing cases of individuals and entire families who have gotten into trouble, and not always through any fault of their own. These people deserve to get a helping hand. Children, for instance, can't help it when their parents don't have any money. Initiatives to do something extra for these children to improve their lives contribute to their positive attitudes later in life. Homeless shelters are for the poorest people in our society; they must be helped. Try to Google projects near you. You'll be amazed at the diversity and the number of initiatives that exist in this field.

It appears that there is a group of people, in the poorest regions of our society, who do not want to improve their own situation. They keep making the same mistakes, they don't adhere to their agreements, promises are made, and broken just as easily, they show little flexibility, give up easily and have a bad temper. The conclusion that these people do not want to be helped is easily drawn. However, often it turns out that they are not unwilling; they are unable. Brain research shows poverty causes a serious emotional and cognitive burden. That burden disrupts the wiring in the brain, causing chronic stress. Stress affects the ability to address problems efficiently, to set priorities and to control impulses. Stress makes it harder to make plans and to achieve long-term goals. In summary: the skills you need to escape from poverty are deteriorated greatly by the stress caused by poverty. Don't forget to help this group out of their vicious cycle.

A Poor Mindset

No true lack of money, but you still feel like you're poor. How is that possible, you might wonder. If only I had millions of Euros in the bank, imagine the things I could do. Imagine these millions in your bank account. This question has been asked before and a lot of people fantasize about a stuffed bank account. This is one of the reasons why lotteries are doing so well. The answers to these questions vary greatly, from traveling to buying a new house or a new car, to going back to school or helping others and quitting the day job. Everyone has their wishes and dreams.

But about that first statement, how can someone with millions in the bank still feel like they're poor? I will explain this based on the example of someone who used to be my employer. He was a successful entrepreneur and was listed in the top 500 of the wealthiest people in the Netherlands. At the time, I was the person financially responsible for his company. Every month, we discussed the figures of the company. As the person who was financially responsible, I learned a lot about the private circumstances of this entrepreneur. He was almost heading for retirement and forwarded a large portion of his capital to his children. After the meeting of his monthly figures, he expressed his greatest concern to me. He felt that, now that he had passed everything on to his children, he was poor and was bound to live on a minimal pension. It took me a couple of sessions to make him see that he had plenty of capital to last him the rest of his life, although he still wasn't entirely convinced. His perception towards money could be classified as a poor mindset.

Solutions for a Poor Mindset

Mindfulness training is the number one way to cure a poor mindset. It's all about looking at money in a new way, recognizing the behaviors and patterns that get you into trouble, and using that awareness to make changes to the ways you interact with money. When we have millions in the bank but see poverty, there's a disconnect happening. The mindset needs to be shifted to get in line with the reality of the situation.

People with a poor mindset do not need charitable donations or a big helping hand. They need to understand the principles of mindfulness—a good exercise for someone in any one of these categories—so they can move forward with a plan to reduce their stress and to feel good about their finances.

You have a say in how your money is to be distributed across pending projects. By installing the Moneyfulness app, reading the daily content and by sharing your opinion, you can earn coins. By sharing these messages, you'll earn extra coins. Participation in discussions at www.Moneyfulness.me and sharing these across various social media will earn you even more. Following the online course is the final opportunity to earn coins. Go to www.Moneyfulness.me to learn about all opportunities for earning and assigning coins.

You can find these coins at www.Moneyfulness.me. Here, you can also find pending projects that currently qualify for sponsoring. The projects are described and may have a video. You can now assign your previously earned coins to a project. Depending on the number of coins assigned, an amount is assigned to various projects. By assigning the coins you earn, you can sponsor projects. Help eliminate poverty through Moneyfulness. Earn your coins and give them to charities.

Chapter 2

MINDFULNESS AND
THE MONEY METHOD

Many folks think they aren't good at earning money,
when what they don't know is how to use it.
–Frank A. Clark

G eorge was always stressed out, especially if he had to pay
someone. He was always shouting at the people he had to
pay, trying to get whatever he could for free. As you can
imagine, George was not a very likable person, all caused by his instant
behavior when his wallet was touched. I met him in a Moneyfulness
workshop, and he was particularly interested in the practical part of
managing his money. His wife sent him, and George wasn't familiar
with mindfulness in the beginning. He didn't realize that his issues with
money stemmed from his mindset until that workshop. It was like a
lightbulb went off. After the Moneyfulness workshop, he also went to a
mindfulness training voluntarily because he immediately recognized the

benefits from the exercises. Now, the moment he feels his anger coming up, he uses the breathing technique he mastered in the mindfulness program and finds a sense of calm again.

Mindfulness has a stress-reducing effect, and it makes you more productive. It adds focus to your thoughts and to your actions. You will enjoy life more, which will make you a lot happier. Mindfulness teaches you to recognize something beautiful in every situation and to enjoy the little things in life. Mindfulness helps you relax and have a more positive image of yourself and your surroundings.

Various studies into stress-related topics clearly show the same three elements: relationships, work and money (and if work concerns retention of your job and with that, your income, this is associated with money).

In the existing mindfulness training sessions, there is plenty of focus on two of the three elements. In the formula of mindfulness, money is not addressed. People who sign up for mindfulness training generally come for anxiety, stress, burnout, or chronic physical complaints. Lack of money or a poor attitude towards money can cause someone great anxiety or stress, which could even lead to depression.

Changing your attitude towards money is the purpose of the Money Method. Everyone has certain beliefs about money. These convictions, have been created somewhere in the past. Perhaps because your parents or others around you voiced their negative opinions of money, saying things like, "Money stinks," Or, "You can't make a silk purse out of sow's ear." Or, "You must keep money moving." Or, "Money doesn't buy happiness."

The other way to build convictions is through your own experiences. In life, you'll go through countless of moments and experiences. If, during your first two jobs, you noticed that doing something extra for your boss leads to promotion or a raise, chances are you will automatically work harder in your third job. If you never saw your hard work pay off in your first two jobs, there is little chance you will work extra hard in your next job.

The Money Method helps you analyze your convictions. Where they come from is not relevant, but they are important to analyze. In particular, when money gives you stress or anxiety, the Money Method will help you understand why so you can address those feelings. As the name suggests, the letters of M-O-N-E-Y represent five steps that will change the way you think about money.

M—Mindset
O—Opportunities
N—Not judging
E—Empowerment
Y—Yourself

Let's take a look at what each letter of the Money Mindset means before we dive into each in later chapters.

Mindset

Moneyfulness begins by questioning your mindset. What is your attitude towards money? It is irrelevant whether you have a lot of money in your account or whether you are in serious overdraft. In this phase, you will map your mindset in an honest way. After all, you are the one who has to face yourself in the mirror tomorrow. To help you with this, you will be given statements and examples. Find out whether you have a poor mindset, have a rich one or are somewhere in the middle. In addition, get to know your poor money characteristics. At the end of this chapter, you will have a mind map of your mindset regarding money.

One of the statements you'll find is: "Rich people may seem happy, but they're not." In other words, you think you know what happens between the ears of rich people. You are the one judging about the happiness of someone else without knowing what actually is going on. Instead, assume that everyone is willing and able to be happy in their own way, regardless of their bank balance.

Opportunities

Opportunities are just around the corner, but you need to start walking to see them. There's a reason why you bought this book. Perhaps you see it as an opportunity to get rid of financial stress or to organize your financial affairs or any other opportunity you saw that convinced you of the added value of this book.

As soon as it concerns money, people suddenly see a lot less opportunity. Suddenly, the road ahead if filled with obstacles. Their brains go in overdrive and they start worrying. Instead of seeing opportunity ahead of them, they only see scarcity. Worrying or contemplating in itself is not a problem. It becomes a problem when you worry a lot and it consumes a part of your day.

If you notice that you frequently worry about money, I have some good news for you. You will start saving a lot of time, which will give you extra time for other fun things. In this phase, you'll turn your negative worries into positive action through four steps.

Not Judging

We're all familiar with the story of *Beauty and the Beast*. An enchantress curses a prince for not showing her kindness when disguised as a beggar, transforming him into a beast. The curse can only be lifted when he is able to love and to be loved by someone else, so long as that happens before a magical rose loses its petals. When Belle first sees the Beast, she, like everyone else, judges him by his appearance and assumes the worst. Part of the enduring allure of the movie is that its themes are universal. We can all identify with the snap judgments the characters make, and we long for the second chances they're lucky enough to get.

We all judge. It makes life more organized, and it allows you to make choices more easily. Be aware of your judgements and which ones you want to change. Moneyfulness is about judgements toward money and your prejudice about others you think either have money— or don't.

Empowerment

Your own strength and your abilities are central in empowerment. Ask yourself whether you are doing the things that make you happy. Are you using your abilities to the fullest? Or are you living someone else's life? Your strengths and abilities can change during life. As a teenager, you most likely had a major social network and easily engaged, but this might be entirely different in your later years. In this life phase, your social network is important for your status and who you are according to your surroundings. You can be or become very good at this. In your thirties and forties, you are working on your career. You have gained experience and you are good at what you do. It feels like you can face the entire world; you get your status from your work. In your fifties and sixties, you might be in search of your inner self, your "being" and the reason for your existence. This is something that happens entirely in yourself, without a large social network.

This is a very crude layout of life phases that people go through. It is an example to show you that your strengths and abilities change throughout your life. For that reason, it is important to look at yourself in the mirror every once in a while and consider whether you are still doing what makes you happy. It is so easy to get dragged into a pattern. You can do something that empowers you right now, and you can keep doing that for quite some time, only to discover after a couple of years that the time has come to close that chapter, because it is consuming more energy than it is giving you. The better you use your abilities, the bigger the chance you can translate it into money. The power of money is greatly underestimated. Find out what your financial abilities are and use them.

Yourself

The last step in the Money Method involves working on yourself. Everything revolves around your mind and your perception of money. In this phase, you will find out what "money type" you are. Based on the eight archetypes, you can see your basic financial behavior. As soon as you know your financial behavior, you'll automatically discover your financial talent and your financial challenges—which money behaviors need to be cultivated and which financial traps you need to avoid. Insight into yourself and your behavior is your foundation for change.

The second part of this chapter contains four neuro-linguistic programming (NLP) techniques. NLP has nothing to do with programming software but with programming your mind. I don't intend to teach you all backgrounds of NLP. Countless of books have been written and countless of courses have been developed on this topic. These four NLP techniques have been included because they will help you manage money and reduce your financial stress. NLP cannot prevent you from having negative experiences in life that make you feel bad. However, NLP can relatively easily teach you to deal with them, to make sure that you feel bad as briefly as possible.

The Money Method Is for Everyone Who Worries about Money

Various studies and questionnaires show that money, relationships and work are the top three of things people stress and worry about. If you have stress about keeping your job, this can be assigned to money. By losing your job, you also lose your income. In fact, you could say everyone worries about money. The majority of people will worry about the lack of money they have and the chunk of month they have left at the end of their money. In addition, there are also people with a significant bank balance, but they too worry about money. They worry about people in their immediate environment who only benefit from their money. They feel stress over the retention of the capital they built singlehandedly. At a certain age, the stress will shift to the inheritance. Has everything been distributed properly? Will my children fight about the inheritance? How can I forward my capital as beneficially as possible, in terms of taxes, etc.?

Your own convictions with regard to money can work for you or against you. As soon as you improve your attitude towards money, you'll be able to make conscious decisions to improve your finances. It might not be visible immediately, but in time, you'll see a difference. By removing obstacles, you clear the road to improvement. So, make sure to get rid of your inhibiting convictions with regard to money and live a happier and better life. Are you not yet ready to get rid of your own convictions and to replace them with a positive conviction? Accept this of yourself and be aware of this conviction. Don't get angry or frustrated with yourself.

Do you worry about financial matters? If so, the Money Method is an added value to your life. With the help of the Money Method, you will gain a more positive attitude and reduce stress with regard to your finances. I won't claim that you will never worry about money or about your financial future ever again, but what I can promise you, is that you will have a different, better attitude towards money after application of the Money Method. Every minute you currently spend on worrying about money can be better utilized for the positive things in life. As you grow up, your parents/caregivers pass on their convictions about money and finances. These are based on what they were taught as a child, combined with their own experiences in life. Chances are, somewhere in previous generations, convictions have been created that used to be useful in the past, but they have not survived the hands of time. The consequences for you are inhibiting convictions in your system. It is time to address these.

With the Money Method, you will get to know yourself better. By increasing your self-knowledge, it will become easier to live with yourself and to do more of what you like and of what you're good at, including financial matters. With this self-knowledge, avoiding your own traps is much easier. Everyone has pitfalls they accidentally step into. Of the eight financial archetypes, I am an Outsider. My pitfall is taking great financial risks. This is evident by the fact that I invested all our savings (and then some) into my company. I invested everything in the online bookkeeping suite and on top of that, I had $45,000 in debt. I could have continued longer, causing my debt to rise. However, nowadays, I have a little voice in my head that warns me of this pitfall.

Applying the Money Method

If you do nothing, nothing will happen. You have already taken the second step in the right direction. You are reading this book, which means you want to change something about your finances or about your attitude towards money. Perhaps, this is because you sense things are not yet as they should be. I can hear you thinking, "What is the first step, then?" Buying this book was the first step. To carry out the Money Method, you need to read the book or attend the online course. What option you choose is not so relevant, as long as you carry out the Money Method.

All changes start with a thought. You realize you want to change something in your life. Then, there are actions towards the picture in your mind of after your change. Imagine plenty of money in your bank account, and you will constantly worry whether it is still in your bank account. In the past, you purchased a safe, and put bills and several gold bars in there. It didn't help, because you still check your bank balance hourly to see whether your money is still in your account. You realize this behavior isn't healthy. It consumes a lot of time and it causes stress to check and guard the capital you earned singlehandedly. You change your mindset to change the habits that consume a lot of time and energy. Without action, there will be no result. If you only think about the desired result without taking any action, then you're dreaming. Dreaming in itself can be great, but dreams will never be reality if no actions are taken.

Money Is Fun and Beautiful

How beautiful is money to you? How about the things you can do with money? A good financial mindset allows you to make your life a lot more beautiful and pleasant. That doesn't mean you have to become a multimillionaire with money to burn. Appreciate the money you have and take good care of it. Everything you nourish will grow. If you want your money to grow, you need to give it the right, positive attention it deserves. If you have a negative mindset about money, you will be worse off financially. You give your attention to the negative side of money, what you nourish will come true.

Spending money on yourself is fun, such as doing pleasant things or buying nice things. Your level of happiness rises significantly when you share your money with others. Giving to charity contributes greatly to your sense of happiness. Giving time and money to charities makes you feel better about yourself, and you become a better person. As your self-esteem grows, the people in your circle will notice, and you'll be able to achieve more. I can go on forever about this, but the point is that you need to find the upward spiral. You need to become the best version of yourself!

Moneyfulness is a process to go through. It consists of exercises that need to be completed. These are exercises that make you question both yourself and your environment. The Money Method is easy but not simple. It is easy to understand but not always easy to carry out.

It requires courage to take a look at yourself and to listen. Digging in your past or becoming aware of your own behavior is a great display of courage.

Think of yourself as an onion. You need to peel yourself layer by layer to reach the core. There are hurdles that can be taken simultaneously. Other hurdles can only be taken one by one. Don't give up too quickly. Persevere, and when you get frustrated, repeat to yourself, "I can do this."

Chapter 3

M–MINDSET

Both poverty and riches are the offspring of thought.
—**Napoleon Hill**

Carol and Peter spent their Friday night on the sofa. Both were exhausted after a week of hard work. As they sat there, Carol wondered how it was possible that they were so drained that all they wanted to do on a Friday night was sit in front of the TV. They used to love playing tennis together and trying out new restaurants. Carol asked Peter what had happened, but nothing in their circumstances had changed. The only thing they could point to was their mindsets.

A mindset can either inhibit or motivate. This sounds extremely simple, but it is very hard. Frequently, failure to change the mindset is discarded with the overly simple answer that you are responsible for your mindset. Identifying the mindset that inhibits you consumes time and energy. This is step one. The second step is to replace your inhibiting mindset with a mindset that motivates you. You mind will make a 180-degree turn. This requires discipline and perseverance. In this chapter, I will help you find your inhibiting mindset with regard to money. The search will reach the deepest parts of your soul. As soon as you have found your inhibiting conviction and the underlying reason of that conviction, you will experience a great sense of freedom. Then, you can start converting your negative feelings into positive energy.

Identifying Your Current Mindset

Upbringing is an important source of convictions. During your youth, you learn a lot and you learn it fast. First-time experiences make a great impression on you. Things that make a great impression affect your convictions. It is not so much about your actions but about the effect of your actions. If you did something that gained you a lot of praise, you have started developing a motivating conviction. You want to experience this positive experience again. It motivates you to repeat this action.

It works exactly the same in reverse. If you said or did something that wasn't received well, the chance is much smaller that you would ever do it again.

Let me tell you about a money theory. It's a theory from about a century ago. Back then, they believed that you were or a spender or a saver. As we'll see soon, there are many more types than that. The theory is that it's determined right after birth if you are a spender or a saver, and it all has to do with poop. As a baby, did you let it all go? Or did you hold it back and it took a long time till your first poop? The quick pooper is a spender and the late pooper is a saver. Now, I can almost hear you laughing, but this theory was developed by none other than Sigmund Freud.

The baby and toddler period is followed by childhood. I would like you to think back to the time when you were somewhere between five and twelve years old. What is your first money memory? Did you get money for your birthday? Did you get pocket money? Were you allowed to do with your money whatever you wanted? Did you have to do household chores in exchange for the money? Or did your parents control you via the pocket money?

What did the people who brought you up tell you over and over? Later, we will go over several examples of what people always used to tell you about money. Let's go through one example here.

If you heard that rich people are "crooks" or "thieves" growing up, you likely imagined something like cartoon villains in masks stealing bags of money from people who need it. As you grow up, that repeated statement shows up in your attitude toward money. Maybe you feel like having too much money is bad or that setting goals to make more money is shallow. But this was before Moneyfulness. If you remember a frequently repeated statement, think about it and see if it holds you back or keeps you down. If it's an inhibiting mindset, change it.

The next phase in life is puberty. You're started to earn more money from your first paid job, and you have more financial responsibilities. Because there are so many firsts at this time of life, you are influenced tremendously by all those first times. Your parents' influence is decreasing, while your friends' opinions become very important. Let's take your first day of your part-time job, for example. You have to fill the shelves in the grocery store. You finished your job early and the owner is busy with the customers. You decide to clean up the warehouse part of the store. Your boss didn't ask you to, but you thought, *It's my first day. Let's make a good impression.*

Now, there are two possible outcomes:

1. Your boss arrives after half an hour in the warehouse at the back of the store and notices what you are doing. He asks if everything he told you to do is done. You tell him you finished about half an hour ago and started to clean the warehouse. Your

boss compliments you on your behavior and pays you more than he should because he was pleased by your initiative.

2. After fifteen minutes of cleaning the warehouse, a colleague walks into the warehouse. He is a full-time employee in the grocery store and the right-hand man to the boss. He starts yelling at you, "Why do you work so hard? Why do you make everyone else look bad?" He's calling you names and keeps on shouting at you for five minutes.

What do you think your attitude will be at your first full-time job? This is the moment your career is starting off. If your experience is the first option, you will probably do something extra your boss doesn't expect. You stand out and get a salary raise or an early promotion. You start earning more money and you will have a shot at a great career. If you experienced the second situation at the age of sixteen or so, you will lay low because you want to keep your job. Your boss doesn't notice you, and there's no salary raise and no promotion for sure.

As you can see, one single moment in your life can affect your entire future. This experience is about making money and making a career, but it can be exchanged for every event during your youth. If your environment motivates you, you will be eager to do more. If your environment takes you down and demotivates you, your life will be different.

The last stage is your adult life. Your mind is set, your neuro pathways are there, and your beliefs don't change that easily anymore. It will take a serious event to change your view on money and your money behavior. For example, a divorce or the death of one of your relatives, which mostly involves an inheritance, may change your views on money. Or maybe it bothers you that you don't live the life you want, and there is an internal motivation to change yourself.

Developing convictions, both inhibiting ones and motivating ones, strongly depends on chance encounters in your environment. There is no good or bad with developing convictions. You simply have a conviction or you don't. What's important right now, is to analyze your convictions about money. This is where Moneyfulness comes in.

12 Statements about Money

To give you a hand, a number of statements are provided below, which you need to complete. Finish the sentence with your conviction. Be honest with yourself in your findings; this is the best and fastest way to map your convictions.

Money makes people _____

Rich people are _____

Poor people are _____

To my father, money was _____

To my mother, money was_____

Within my family, money was _____

To my partner, money is _____

If I had more money, I would _____

When I have money, I usually spend it on _____

When I have money, I am _____

If I had more money, I would be afraid that _____

Money is _____

After you have finished all 12 statements with your own experience and convictions, read them all thoroughly. In particular, pay attention to negative tendencies. Where do these negative convictions come from? Don't expect to have an answer to this question, but thinking about it will help you begin gaining insight into your inhibiting convictions.

Convictions

People can be divided into three groups when it comes to money-related convictions. Your bank balance is separate from your convictions. You might have a lot of money in the bank and still have the money-related convictions of a poor person. In the following three paragraphs, I will show you examples of three types of convictions. The mirror you need to look in shows you what group you're currently in. While you may identify with two groups, try to see what group you can identify with most. I'll walk you through examples of each conviction type. There is no good or bad in this, only an observation of your current convictions. The goal is to help you get rid of your inhibiting convictions.

Convictions of the "Bottom Mass"

If wealth is a ladder, I am near the bottom of it. In my teens and early twenties, I went to school. I was awarded a diploma, and that was about it for me. Sometimes I feel like I'm the victim of my own life. I don't really worry; the government takes care of me. I make money by working. I am given money in return of my time. I spend almost all the money I make, because what's the point of saving? Well, I do save a little for my vacations, but after my vacation, all my savings are gone. Money is a scarce commodity and time is something I have plenty of. My retirement plan is taken care of by my employer, and I don't have to do anything extra for that. Climbing the ladder and getting rich? That will only happen if I win the grand prize in a lottery or when I turn out to have an unknown rich family member who leaves me money.

Convictions of the "Middle Ground"

My most important diplomas were awarded to me in my teens and twenties. Afterwards, I mainly attended separate courses. These courses allowed me to climb the corporate ladder. I feel that I have plenty of time and I don't mind exchanging this time for money. I am responsible for myself and my family, but I have little control of the government and the economy in general. Together with my employer, I save up for my retirement. After retirement, I don't want to cut back on my expenses; I want to keep living like I'm doing now. That is why, for a period of 40 years, I put away a monthly amount, so that I can keep living this life after my retirement. In addition to fun things and vacations, I spend my money on financial obligations, such as a house and a more expensive car. I currently have a 3-month buffer. Should something happen, I can keep living like this for 3 months without having to worry. In addition to hoping for the jackpot, I expect to have a significant amount in my bank account before retiring. That's what I'm truly targeting for.

Convictions of the "Rich"

Leaning and attending training is something that I will do for the rest of my life. As soon as I stop learning, I'll stop growing. I control my financial life, and I take full responsibility for that. I create money systems and invest. The aim is to make money work for me. I have sufficient direct buffers to be financially secure, and I invest the rest. I want to be financially independent as soon as possible. This gives me a sense of freedom. I spend my money on possessions, companies, real estate, training, etc. My goals in life are to build systems and to invest. The assets will become as big as possible, as soon as possible. Time is a scarce commodity; I handle it carefully.

Fantasies, Dreams, and Goals

The convictions of the bottom mass, middle ground and rich show you how these groups deal with money. The bottom mass can only fantasize about winning the jackpot. Fantasizing about what to do with all that money, should you win it, is wonderful. However, the chance of actually winning is smaller than the chance of being hit by lightning. The mindset of this group can be described as fantastical, not realistic. The middle ground dreams of a pension, saving for 40 years, to be able to enjoy the accrued capital after retirement. They dream of all great things they can do once they reach retirement. The fear in this is whether the saved capital is enough to survive your entire pension. The question of the middle ground with regard to dreams is, to be able to realize it, you have to wait 40 years for it, and when the time comes, will it be enough? A rich mindset is characterized by the control and responsibility you take of your own life and your own financial situation. The government and the uncertain future are given less trust by this group. Goals are set to be able to live independently from others. The mindset of this group is about setting and achieving goals.

What mindset can you most identify with? Again, right now, we are simply identifying your mindset as it is.

Statements about Money

The following exercise, which is about your mindset with regard to money, consists of a number of statements. The trick is to find the statements that best suit you. They consist of a large number of negative, inhibiting convictions. Try to find the five main inhibiting convictions and circle the ones you identify with. Try to circle no more than five convictions to work on.

1. When I have a lot of money, I may lose it.
2. When I look deep into my heart, I don't have to be rich.
3. You need money to make money.
4. Money can cause a lot of trouble.
5. If you have a lot of money, you are cheap.
6. Money is not that important.

7. With great money comes great responsibility.
8. Getting rich is a matter of being lucky.
9. Money is the root of all evil.
10. Realistically speaking, there is little chance of me getting rich.
11. Getting rich is nothing for people like me.
12. When I get rich, everyone will want something from me.
13. The rich have apparently done something bad and dishonest to make their money.
14. I am too young/too old to get rich.
15. I am not educated enough to get rich.
16. I don't have the time to manage my money.
17. I wish there was no such thing as money.
18. I don't need to manage my money, since I hardly have any.
19. It is not fair that I'm rich, whereas others aren't.
20. Rich people are rarely happy.
21. If I get rich, that's fine; if I don't, that's fine too.
22. I hate bearing responsibility.
23. I am repulsed by rich people.
24. It is better to be paid for my time than for what I do.
25. It's all good; I don't need to push myself.
26. When you're wealthy in terms of love, health and happiness, you don't need money.
27. I can do it on my own; I don't need others.
28. When I ask for help, people will think that I'm weak.
29. The only reason to work is to make money.
30. I am simply not destined to be rich.
31. Investing is only for rich people with a lot of money.
32. Most investments, other than a bank account, are too risky.
33. Getting rich is too much work and hassle for me.
34. I don't feel good enough to be rich.
35. The goal to get rich leaves little time for other things.

36. Having a lot of money means being less spiritual and pure.
37. When I have a lot of money, it means that someone else has less.
38. I am simply not good at money and finances.
39. I could potentially get rich, but I need a break right now.
40. Working on my financial future is a little inconvenient right now.
41. It is not fair to make more than my parents.
42. People should not have more money than they need to survive.
43. The pursuit of riches causes stress and health issues.
44. Most great opportunities have already been seized.
45. I am not smart or intelligent enough to get rich.
46. I don't like managing my money.
47. Money corrupts the artistic, creative and sportive world.
48. I am too busy to invest time and energy in my financial knowledge.
49. There's no point in making more money; it only means I have to pay more taxes.
50. I'm already quite comfortable; I don't need to push myself.
51. By getting rich, I will prove myself to the rest of the world.
52. Getting rich is not a skill.

Which five of these 52 statements best matches your feelings and emotions? If you read a statement and it immediately resonated with you, that might be one of them. Remember to choose no more than five convictions. This is a tool to find your inhibiting convictions with regard to money, and you want to start by focusing on the five strongest convictions you hold.

10 Bad Money Characteristics

Everyone has good and bad characteristics, and that's no different when it concerns money. Good characteristics must be treasured; bad characteristics are best converted into good ones, or eliminated altogether. These 10 bad money characteristics are the final tool to revealing your inhibiting convictions. After these 10 money characteristics, you'll work on the findings you observed up to here. Circle all that apply to you.

1. Not managing your money. By not paying any attention to your money, you tell it that it is not important. Whether you want it or not, money is important in this day and age.

2. Not saving. By spending all your money and not saving, you are unable to build buffers, let alone to invest. It is not about the amount; it is about putting it aside.

3. The habit to make debt. When you keep making new debt, you'll only be working on repaying it. You never will be able to save. Take note of how vulnerable you are in this society.

4. Living above your paygrade means spending more than you make. As soon as there are buffers, this doesn't have to be a problem. You can simply choose to consume your buffers. You may have even created a buffer in the past for that reason. However, in the long term, this is a serious problem.

5. Not developing yourself financially. If you have saved money, you can invest. Putting money in the bank hardly yields any return. Investing in something you don't know anything about is not smart.

6. Following unsound advice. In the world of investments, there are plenty of ignorant consultants and consultants with interest that don't match yours. Choose your consultant carefully.

7. As soon as your income rises, your expenses will rise as well. An increase in income is the perfect moment to increase a buffer or to start saving for future investments. In principle, your expenses don't rise when your income rises.

8. Not asking what you're worth. Whether you work for a company or are an entrepreneur, stop thinking in hourly rates. Ask what you're worth. How much is someone willing to pay for your services? Make sure you get paid what you're worth.

9. Never negotiating. If you never negotiate, you'll always pay too much. You can't negotiate about everything, but you can negotiate about a lot.

10. Wasting your time. There is so much distraction nowadays, so wasting time is easy to do. Think about what is important for you and for your environment. Work on your priorities and try to be distracted as little as possible.

Do you recognize yourself in one or more of these 10 characteristics? Include them in the process of changing your own mindset with regard to money.

Dig Deeper

You have now gathered a number of points from the aforementioned exercises with regard to your inhibiting convictions about money. It is important to pick the most relevant points from every exercise. Write these points on a sheet of paper. For every element, write the first thought that comes to mind about where this inhibiting conviction or behavior comes from. What causes it? This exercise demands a lot from your memory and from your emotions. You need to dig deep into your soul to see why you have these feelings or why you do the things you do. With the help of these exercises, you have peeled off the outer layers. By asking yourself these questions, you reach the core of your convictions. Spend plenty of time and attention on analyzing the outcomes of your exercises. The better you do this and the deeper you dig, the sooner and easier you'll be able to leave it behind you.

The Mind Map

A tool to organize your thoughts and to analyze your previous findings is a mind map. In a mind map, you visually represent your thoughts. You place the topic in the center and everything related to it around it. Using lines, you can specify connections between main topics and sub-topics. Using different letters and colors, you can specify what is important and what isn't. This contributes to the thinking process, giving you better insight into your convictions with regard to money, resulting in a clear overview of previously collected thoughts and details. You can create your mind map on a large sheet of paper and draw all kinds of lines and connections between source thoughts and associations. Online, you can find various digital tools for making a mind map. Use the tool that suits you best.

Put yourself in the center, consider yourself—to use mind map wording—a project. You want to find out what convictions and characteristics you have with regard to money. Place all convictions and characteristics you have found around yourself. See if there are any overlapping convictions/behaviors or characteristics and convictions that are related. Connect these by drawing lines between matching convictions. Write the feelings and ideas you have with every conviction. The next step is to take these feelings and ideas, and to come up with situations from your past that might have shaped this conviction or characteristic. Do this for every individual conviction. Then, connect matching feelings, ideas and situations from the past. Chances are, you will be shifting around the shapes and lines you have now. By using the mind map, you can organize and gain insight into your own thoughts and behavior with regard to money. Now you know what you have to work on. Either you quit displaying this behavior, or you convert your inhibiting conviction into a motivating conviction. You are the person at the helm of your own mindset. Your thoughts are yours and nobody else's. This is when you decide how the future will be different.

Time Is Money

Time is money. If you have an inhibiting mindset, you feel like you have more time than money. When you have a rich mindset, you are convinced that time has much more value than money. The generally applicable statement, time equals money, is middle ground. It is time to analyze how you spend your time. If you assume that time is worth much more than money, you will feel that you must spend your time wisely. As the American entrepreneur Jim Rohn says, "You can make more money, but when you're out of time, you're done." It is not (yet) possible to use your money to buy extra time. Focus on things that are important to you and make time for them. Stop wasting time, and find out what you spend your time on. Are your activities useful, or do they simply make time pass but contribute nothing of value?

Imagine a rat in a cage. There is a treadmill in the cage. Without external motivation, the rat will get on the treadmill and start walking. At first, the rat will walk slowly, but gradually, it will have to walk faster, until it has to run. After a while, it will be drained and exhausted, but the treadmill keeps going and it can't get out. When you allow people to do this, it is referred to as burnout. Still, this is how our career society works. You slowly start working and you build a career. You start walking faster, making more money. Instead of putting money aside, you start spending more. Now, you need to run faster to have money to spend, so you need to build a better career, rise faster on the corporate ladder, work more, make more, and spend more. There will be a point when you ask yourself how you can escape from this rat race. It isn't easy, because this is when your ego surfaces. How do you see yourself? How do others see you, and how do you want to be seen?

This is your mindset, change it and you will be able to take leaps in the right direction.

Summary Mindset
- Get to know your own mindset with regard to money.
- Answer the twelve statements about money.
- What statements did you answer negatively?
- Do you have the convictions of the rich, the poor, or somewhere in between?
- Choose the top five statements about money you can most identify with (no more than five).
- Which of the ten bad money characteristics apply to you?
- Make a mind map of your mindset with regard to money.
- Take these answers to the next chapters on the Money Method.

The next chapter is about opportunities. See opportunities, recognize them and seize them.

Chapter 4
O–OPPORTUNITIES

I never want money to dictate what I can and can't do in life
—**Jessica Moorhouse**

Two colleagues are catching up at the coffee machine, sharing the latest gossip. In the existing team, another colleague has been promoted to boss of their department. The two colleagues are wondering out loud why this rookie was given this job. What track record does he have? The two feel that he hasn't earned it yet. In the evening, both colleagues go home and discuss the promotion they missed with their partners. Why was he given this opportunity instead of me? They can't stop thinking about it; the thought won't leave their minds. The result: another sleepless night and another tired day at work.

You are reading this book, which gives you the opportunity to change and improve your attitude towards money. Opportunities are everywhere. What's important is that you learn to see and seize opportunities. Seeing opportunities is difficult if you are doing a thousand things simultaneously, each thing serving a different goal. They're also quite difficult if you're distracted by the opportunities given to other people, as in our example above. If your focus is elsewhere, you are likely to miss this opportunity.

Another important reason why people miss opportunities is fear and the desire to stay within your own comfort zone. Yes, your comfort zone may feel safe and familiar, but outside your comfort zone is where all the fun and exciting things happen. And of course you may have, at one point, considered something an opportunity only to find out it wasn't. That doesn't mean it was wrong. At least you tried, and you can never blame yourself for being too passive. You can't fail; you can only learn and grow.

Financial opportunities don't present themselves by chance. Your focus needs to be on your goal to increase your income. If you actively look for a new job with a higher salary, one of these jobs is bound to present itself at some point. Investing works exactly the same. If you are looking for investment opportunities, a proposition will present itself in due time. It is up to you to seize these opportunities.

Worrying as a Habit

Worrying is a necessary evil. This isn't a pleasant feeling, but it helps you discover what needs to be fixed. As long as you don't spend more than 5 minutes worrying, there's no problem. Observe and register what it is you worry about. When the topic of your worrying pops up frequently, it is time to do something about it. Spending hours at night worrying about money issues is not a good habit. Nor is staring at your computer screen for hours during the day, worrying how to get through the rest of the month. Are you a notorious worrier, and do your worries cost you a ton of time during the day or night? If so, schedule half an hour to an hour a day to worry. In this time, have all topics pass review about which you want to worry and write them down. Forbid yourself from worrying about topics outside your worry-time if they have passed reviewed. Allow yourself time to worry but limit the time during which you do so.

Worrying is a dialogue that takes place in your mind. You are the one controlling the voices in your head. This can lead to huge mental noise—a cacophony of noises and conversations. Everyone frequently runs a dialogue through their mind to help them visualize situations. However, as soon as the dialogues in your mind (the worrying) gets the upper hand during the day, you suffer. If you spend nights awake, it is time to do something about it. Bad nights like these have an effect throughout the day. Dialogues in your brain keep on going. This puts you in a negative spiral from which it is very hard to escape. It can literally make you ill.

Worrying can consume your entire day. Your brain is the biggest energy consumer of your body. Knowing this, you can imagine that worrying consumes a ton of energy. Because you spend your energy and valuable time on worrying, you have no time left for the daily activities you have to perform. If you worry a lot about your debt, and this keeps you occupied throughout the day, this adversely affects your work. This leads to the risk of losing your job and your income. This, in turn, results in more stress and more things to worry about. Time is a scare commodity, so handle it wisely. Worrying only has added value to a limited extent. Worrying day and night has no added value at all. Imagine what it would be like if you spent all your worrying time and energy in a good way. What would you be able and willing to do with all that time and energy?

How to Stop Worrying

To be able to convert your worrying time and energy into positive energy and action, you must first break through a negative spiral. There are a number of ways to do so.

1. Make sure your house is clutter-free and calm. A clutter-free house contributes to a clutter-free mind. Without distraction, you'll be able to better focus on your task.

2. Exercise. Literally get the unrest out of your body. It doesn't matter whether you exercise in a gym, start running outside or simply choose to walk for a while; exercise frees your mind.

3. Mindfulness meditation. Within mindfulness, there are many exercises to ease your mind. Use them. Meditating is one step further for a lot of people, but it can also be very helpful.

4. Don't make it bigger than it is. Write down the things you worry about and assess how big of a disaster it would be if these things actually happened.

5. Overdue small tasks. Your to-do list probably contains a lot of things that don't consume a lot of time. Schedule several hours to get these small tasks done. This helps you cut your to-do list in half, and in doing so, the unrest in your head will diminish as well.

6. Talking. If your worrying issue is so big that you can't resolve it yourself, go talk to someone. Others have a neutral position with respect to your thoughts. From this neutral position, others can help you break your negative spiral.

7. Healthy distraction. Do something to get your mind off things so you can relax. Using alcohol and drugs as an escape is not an option in this. Do something fun, like gardening, taking a nap, going to the movies, etc.

Your thoughts determine how you feel. You decide what happens. Disappointments in life are inevitable, and worrying won't help you avoid them. Accept that not everything goes the way you would like to, and not everything you try will succeed. Worrying about failures in the past amounts to nothing. There are no failures if you learned from the experience or grew as a person because of it. Try to get something positive from every disappointment. Take one topic you worry about, or more, and write something positive next to it. Analyzing how your debt came to be and how you got into this mess is useful, but only once. Accept this behavior from the past and build your future.

Turning Energy Around

The feeling associated with disappointment and failure is not pleasant. It temporarily drains your energy, because all your energy is invested in processing and mulling over your disappointment. It is important to get your energy to a higher level. Take the list of things you worry about and organize them from "catastrophic" to "it's not so bad." Rigorously strike through the bottom half. Worrying about these topics is not worth your time or energy. Next to all topics that remain, write the ideal positive outcome. Coming up with a positive outcome in your mind is a powerful way to turn energy around and to stop worrying. Visualize the positive outcome of dialogues in your mind, add one or more of the five sense to them, and the topic you used to worry about will now give you energy. In this way, you can quickly turn your energy level around, from low to high.

The same structure can also be applied to the bills you need to pay. If you pay later, what creditor will give you the most trouble, and what creditor won't mind as much? Pay attention to the amounts. Let's say that twenty bills need to be paid. Of these twenty bills, fifteen have a low amount, two are average and three are big amounts. If these bills are equally important, it is better to pay five small amounts than one big one. Every bill, regardless of the amount, gives you stress. It is better to eliminate five stress factors than one. When you are truly in default, this method can help you climb out of the hole and convert your debt into possessions. In the end, all bills need to be paid.

A long time ago, Albert Einstein claimed that energy does not dissipate; it only relocates. The same goes for money, it does not disappear; it relocates. Imagine how the money will move in your direction. Science is more and more focused on the phenomenon that everything is energy and that energy does not dissipate. Everything on this Earth is built from molecules and atoms. Atoms and molecules are constantly in motion. Motion requires energy. "Thoughts are energy" is the next logical step. How you think determines how energy flows. If you think in opportunities, opportunities will actually present themselves. If you go to a supermarket on a busy Saturday afternoon with the conviction that you will find a parking spot, chances are you will actually find one.

Everything you give attention will grow. Attention can be both positive and negative. When you think about worrying, worrying is what you will do. That is why you should focus your energy and thoughts on positive matters. The best thing is to take a topic you worry about, turn around your energy and attitude, and after a while, get the outcome of the positive scenario you came up with. You have given the positive scenario the attention it deserved. Give your money the attention it deserves. Imagine a positive inbound stream of money.

Changing Your Perspective

By changing your thoughts and your perspective, your view of the world changes as well. By separating main issues from side issues, you will be able to paint yourself a clear picture. You will go back to the core of yourself. From yourself, changing you is not the intention; you are very well aware of what matters to you and what you value. By putting your focus, attention and energy on truly important matters, you can realize your goals. By eliminating all side issues, you can remove a lot of noise. Every time you eliminate a side issue, your view will become clearer. Look inside your heart to see what matters to you, and focus on that.

Seeing Opportunities

John Gardner, author of *James Bond*, expressed seeing opportunities in a great way. Opportunities are often wonderfully disguised as problems that can't be solved. You have a good thing going on, and all your energy and thoughts are focused on one topic. You have a goal in mind that you wish to achieve. You run into a problem. No matter how you look at the problem, it seems like you can't get around or over it.

Your subconscious then gets to work, looking for solutions to the problem that can't seem to be solved. After a while, you suddenly get an idea, and you see the light, the solution to your problem. Don't give up too quickly, and give your subconscious an opportunity to present the solution. As soon as you have overcome this roadblock, the road to your future is paved. The opportunity to realize your goal is clearer than ever. The solution that came from your subconscious can be so creative that it results in a huge opportunity.

The story of the invention of the Post-it by Art Fry is such a moment. Fry was getting increasingly frustrated about the bookmarks that kept falling out of his choir book. Because of his frustration about the pesky bookmarks, his subconscious went looking for a solution to the falling bookmarks. In a *Eureka!* moment, he allegedly got the idea of using adhesives for his bookmarks. 3M made this idea big with Post-its. Art Fry had a problem, and it resulted in a major solution. What are your problems with money? Where do you see financial opportunities? Frequently put these questions in your subconscious and wait for an answer.

Blurred Perspective

Taking time to stop and reflect does not fit will in our hectic society. We generally run from one thing to another. Because you take so little time to stop and reflect, you don't know what truly matters to you, and you are doing way too many things at once. Someone with dozens of priorities has no clear vision. They may find that they have seized many opportunities and achieved a great deal but those goals weren't theirs. They were someone else's idea of success that they never stopped to question or evaluate.

Shanon came to Chicago in 2012. He had just been awarded his master's degree in law and wanted to proceed to earn a Ph.D. To get his Ph.D. he had to borrow $36,000. Because he and his parents were so proud, he thought this was what he wanted, but after having worked for a year, he found out that law wasn't his thing at all.

He showed guts and followed his dream: working in an animal shelter. He realized too late that he had taken out a loan for a dream he didn't really want. His debt remained, so he rolled up his sleeves and created a nice life for himself, keeping his expenses to only $750 per month. After Shanon paid back his debt, he kept living creatively like this. This lifestyle has resulted in him being financially independent, fifteen years later. By failing to stop and think about his own goals and by rushing into his studies, his perspective was temporarily blurred. Fortunately, he was able to turn it around.

Setting Goals

Opportunities present themselves when you have clear goals. Concretize the goals you set. Some goals may be easier to solidify than others. A tool in setting goals is the SMART theory.

The letters represent:

- Specific: Is your objective clear and unambiguous?
- Measurable: With which values has your goal been achieved? By this, I mean absolute numbers.
- Acceptable: Is the goal acceptable for everyone?
- Realistic: Is the goal must feasible?

- Time-bound: The goal must have an end date. This is the final moment to see whether the goal was achieved.

To help you get started, to get your creativity flowing, the areas below are for setting goals. This should serve as a guide. This list is not exhaustive; there are a lot of possibilities for setting goals.

1. Financial goal: How much do you want to make in the year to come? Do you want to have your debt repaid? How much would you like to have invested at the end of the year?
2. Professional goal: Would you still like to have the same job? Would you like to start as an entrepreneur?
3. Goal relationship and friendships: Are you still friends with the same people? Do you want to improve your relationship with someone? Are you looking for a role model?
4. Health goal: How often and how much will you work out? Will you start eating healthier? Would you like to lose a certain amount of weight?
5. Goal in personal development: What training will you follow? Will you look for a mentor?
6. Charities: How much do you want to give to charity this year? What will you work for as a volunteer?

In Moneyfulness, the first and last goals are focused on the most. They have to do with increasing your income and reducing your expenses. Think of an amount and a time on which you want to have this amount. Every day, tell yourself out loud: "On _____, I want to have _____. This money will come in in various amounts, depending on the extent to which I deliver my goods or services." Provide a clear focus on the financial goal.

In achieving your financial goal, think about how much of it you want to donate to charities. This can be an absolute amount or a percentage of the accrued capital as of that date. Later in this book, you will read more about the reciprocity of giving and the happiness giving brings you, including scientific substantiation.

Seizing Opportunities

One thing is for sure: opportunities will present themselves. But how do you actually seize opportunities? Give your subconscious space to come up with creative solutions. As soon as an idea presents itself, don't hesitate to carry out the idea as quickly as possible. The most beautiful and best ideas are outside of your comfort zone. That's what's so great about opportunities: they give you energy and butterflies. Do new things, do different things, do the same things a different way—do everything to get you out of your rut. Don't get frustrated when some time goes by without new ideas popping into your head. Don't count on inventing the new Post-it. Wait patiently and ideas will present themselves. Don't be too hard on yourself; you have your surroundings for that.

Everything begins with a good idea. Your thoughts focus on the good idea to give it the attention and energy it deserves. Visualize that you realized your idea. Add a good feeling to this visualization. How cool is it to have your idea visualized? By visualizing the realization of your idea and feeling good about it, the ideas to realize it will present themselves automatically. This is the "how" of your idea. An idea in itself is nothing, but as soon as you know how to realize the idea, you will have arrived at the next step: carrying out the idea. Don't try to detail all steps from idea to realization in the beginning. Start with a first small step, and then quickly proceed to the second small step. There's no need to have step 10 all detailed when you're still working on step one. As long as the direction and the end goal are clear, keep moving towards the eventual goal. As long as you keep moving, realization moves closer. You will go from thoughts to feelings, and these thoughts and feelings are then converted into action, and eventually, you will achieve the result.

Start paying off your debt. If it takes small steps in the beginning, that's no problem, as long as you keep taking steps. As soon as your debts are repaid, you can begin building capital. It is not about the absolute amount; taking steps, and continuing to do so towards your goal, is what matters most.

Summary Opportunities
Deal with worrying in a constructive way.

- Use the seven ways to break the negative spiral.
- Everything is energy, so turn negative energy into positive energy.
- Set goals for yourself and make these goals SMART.
- Determine the six different goals you set for yourself.
- Go from thoughts to results; that's how you do it.

Don't judge, and don't condemn. What should you look for and what should you do if you judge too quickly and share that with others? This is what the next chapter is all about.

Chapter 5

N–NOT JUDGING

Too many people spend money they haven't earned, to buy things they don't want, to impress people they don't like.
—Will Rogers

With the rise of social media, venting your opinion has become easier and more customary. Judgement is often passed online in an unfiltered manner. Unfortunately, making a snap judgement doesn't mean you have better insight. The snap judgement is nothing more than a repetition of your existing thoughts. It leaves no room for new insights and new ideas. It is more important to find the reason why you form judgement so quickly. That is when room can be made for new ideas and new insights.

Check the list of 52 statements about money in Chapter 3 once more. This list deliberately contains various judgements and prejudices. What do your top five look like? Did any stand out to you? Did you immediately picture anyone after reading some of them?

We simplify our world by judging, by putting information into categories. Simplifying information is a way to process information faster. It's interesting to see and feel what response is triggered by your prejudice. What effect does the judgement have on you? Does it involve status? Does it give you extra attention? What response do you get on your judgement and what response do you expect from the group? This sounds very dramatic, but it can be substantiated with a very simple example. Imagine stepping into a room with nothing but people you don't know. You look around the room with 15 others who don't know each other. You see someone with an angry look on his face. Within a second, your brain forms an opinion about this person. Chances are slim that you would engage someone with an angry face in conversation. You will never know whether this stranger just ate something sour, causing the face you saw. You just don't know.

This works in reverse, too. Knowing others will make snap judgments, we try to influence those judgments to make sure they are positive. You never get a second chance to make a first impression. This is the main reason why you dress so nicely on your first date. You want to make a good first impression on the other; you want their snap judgement of you to be a positive one.

Will Rogers' quote hits the mark. Try walking through your house and look at all your stuff. Don't forget the attic, because that's where everything ends up that you don't want to throw away, but you don't use either. You'll probably find items there that you once purchased to impress someone else. If you made such a useless purchase, ask yourself whom you bought this for. Hopefully, it was a fun person at least. This chapter explains how to make good decisions with you in mind. This means tuning out your judgments of others, focusing on yourself, and cultivating a better mindset about money so you can start to repay debt, build a savings buffer, and maybe start to invest.

Financial Judgements

It's easy to judge the financial situation of someone else. Look at your neighbor: he just bought a very big and expensive car, so he must be doing great. Every week, he goes out to dinner to a very expensive restaurant. How about that acquaintance who lives in a large house? He must be doing really well and be really successful. Or that friend of mine, an entrepreneur, who is always on the news and has such great stories—he must be a successful entrepreneur. All these examples have to do with a certain form of status. Imagine someone receiving an inheritance or a huge amount in a lottery. This allows a person to buy houses and cars and to go to expensive restaurants. If there is no inheritance or lottery, perhaps there is no money at all. Perhaps this person is almost broke but tries to keep up appearances, or even worse, launches himself into debt. This is how easy it is to judge someone's financial situation by only looking at appearances. Everyone has their own wallet and uses it as they please. Only look at your own wallet, and don't judge the expenses of others, especially when you have no idea about the income or capital of the other. An incorrect judgement is passed all to easily.

Stereotypes

A stereotype is an exaggerated image of a group of people that often does not match reality. It is a prejudice or negative thought, and it is often used to justify certain discriminatory actions. Thinking in stereotypes is in line with judging. You label people, like "dumb blondes" or "video-game nerds." Or worse. It would be easy to name a long list of stereotype examples here. Think about the stereotypes you have in your mind. These are mainly groups of people who are outside your comfort zone. The further they are outside your comfort zone, the easier it is to have an opinion about them. You don't know these people, so you can say about them what you want without any problems. Spreading your stereotype judgements reaches these group, so you end up harming them after all. These stereotypes feed the way we judge others on their finances.

Other people have expectations of you; at least, that's what you think. You are part of a group, or you wish to be part of one, meaning you start behaving according to the expectations of others. If you no longer meet the expectation of others, you are rejected from the group. This already begins in elementary school among small children, and it continues throughout life. The strongest sense of group importance lives among adolescents. If, as an adolescent, you behave differently than the rest, you are out before you know it. When that happens, it is nearly impossible to join another group. It means that you would have to adopt all their opinions. Among adolescents, this is so strong that their clothing tells you what group they belong in. Within a group, there's a hierarchy, in which the most important person dictates the opinion of the group. After puberty, it slowly gets easier for people to form their own opinions. That doesn't mean it gets easier to let go of expectations of others though. Try to let go of your expectations of others. Others do not have to behave according to your standards. Be aware of the fact that your way is not the best way; it is just a way. There's always more than one way leading to Rome.

Try Not to Change Others

Others change, and imposing your opinion is not a good way to get them to change. Don't try to change others, allow everyone to form their own opinion. You can however inspire people. If you do this, you are expressing your opinions in a very enthusiastic manner. There's nothing wrong with this. Be inspired by others. Listen to others, because there's always something to learn. Other people have other insights; it is up to you to form your own judgement about the other and what he or she has to say. Don't judge them but use their insights to form your opinion. Other insights help you to see the situation from different angles, allowing you to form a more objective opinion. Enjoy people as they are and leave them be. If the whole world would adjust to your opinions, Earth would be a very boring place.

Practice judging and improving your response to your own judgement is associated with a number of focus points. For starters, it is good to only have topics in your mind that are related to your conversation or your interlocutor (no unrelated thoughts allowed). Be alert during the conversation, focused on the conversation because if you're not, your perspective will be blurry, or you will miss parts of the conversation altogether. Take your time with it; you want to be able to hear the other person. Be interested and curious, and whatever you do, don't interrupt the other person. Confirming nods contribute to communication. During the story, you are not yet allowed to form an opinion about the contents of the story. There will automatically be room in the conversation for asking questions. Ask open questions to allow the other to further explain where necessary. Ask questions to obtain information, and only after the conversation. Make sure that, after the conversation, you have enough information, and conduct further research if necessary. You have now formed your opinion and it is alright if you disagree with the other. Not agreeing is not your judgement but it does say something about your judgement. Make sure that your judgement is based on multiple perspectives of the same story.

You Don't Know Someone Else's Story

You meet someone at a certain point in their life. At that moment, you only see the end result of all preceding years, experiences and events. In fact, you only see a small portion of the end result; events that have already been processed are no longer visible, so you only see signs of them. For instance, someone who comes across as very dominant, may come from a history of being bullied. People who talk a lot about themselves may be looking for acknowledgement that they never received from their parents. What voices are still present in your mind? What people are you eager to label to give them a place that originates from your fears and insecurities? Even if you think you know someone, you still only see the tip of the iceberg. A human life has endless nuances and complications. There isn't an opinion in the world that does justice to the person in front of you.

From the outside, you see the tip of the iceberg. You can't blindly rely on the outside, because you don't know what happens behind the front door. What happens in someone's mind is a mystery for someone on the outside. Someone may have nice capital at the moment or a good income, but you don't know what path they traveled to get there. A great example of that is the movie *The Pursuit of Happyness*, starring Will Smith and his son. After a night in a holding cell, he is miraculously accepted to a traineeship for stockbrokers. The traineeship is unpaid. His fellow trainees do not know that he sleeps in a homeless shelter and has no roof over his head. They even spend a night in the restroom of a Subway station. This is not the prevailing image of a stockbroker. Eventually, he is hired as a stockbroker and has a bright future awaiting him. The financial situation of Will Smith's character was invisible to others. They did not know his story.

You will form opinions and judge throughout your life. It would be unrealistic to think that you could live without judging. You can however change the way you judge. How you judge others says much more about you than it does about them. Your judgements and prejudices expose how you think about yourself and your environment. Analyzing your prejudices equals looking into the mirror. You'll find where your fears and insecurities are. You use your judgments to label your insecurities and fears. When you feel good about yourself, you approach others from a place of compassion and interest. When you approach someone like that, there is much less to judge. In this case, it simply is what it is, and you can usually leave it at that. By judging less negatively, you can enjoy all people around you to a more optimal extent. All people are different and have other ideas. Accept that others have their own ideas and judgments. Look at them and learn from them.

Feel free to be who you are. Based on the ideas, opinions and inspiration of others, you can form your own opinion. Don't force your opinion onto others. Don't be so concerned with the life of others; just live your own. You sell yourself short when you get too invested in the lives of others. Know that everyone is different, and you don't have to have an opinion about everything. Allow others to make their own life journey. If you have no opinion about that, life is much more peaceful and relaxed. You don't have to worry about others, needlessly spending negative energy. That doesn't mean that you have to start ignoring others entirely. You can listen to others without judging and help them in doing so. You can get inspiration from others in a positive way. You don't have to become apathetic. The idea is to no longer condemn and to judge people and everyday events less and to refrain from taking immediate action or venting your judgement.

Your own financial situation is the most important. Shield yourself from the appearances of others. Spend your money on things that are important to you. If someone else eats at five-star restaurants or has a more expensive car than you, then that is his or her choice. It may be that someone else has more money to spend than you do, but from the outside, it is impossible to see whether that other is knee-deep in debt as a result of their spending pattern.

Summary Not Judging
- About what do you form snap judgements?
- Focus points when judging.
- Everyone judges; the trick is to deal with it wisely.
- Discover your financial prejudices/judgements.
- Focus on yourself and judge as little as possible.
- You only see the tip of the iceberg.

Empowerment is a concept that is used frequently nowadays in various meanings. In the next chapter, you'll find out what meaning Moneyfulness attributes to empowerment.

Chapter 6

E-EMPOWERMENT

Do what you love, and the money will follow.
—Marsha Sinetar

Y ou wouldn't believe it if I told you, which is why I will show you an example of someone who took action and empowered herself. It is the story of Abigail and her husband. Both Abigail and her husband suffer from health issues. When she was 19, Abigail almost died from a rare neurological disorder. As a result of her illness, she thought that she could never find work and that her husband would need to stay home to care for her.

Everybody has capacities, and so does Abigail.

At their ultimate low point, their debt amounted to $45,000. A combination of illness, disability, unemployment and debt don't form a recipe for a happy, prosperous life. They were miserable.

Then, they decided to change course. Abigail went through the house and sold everything they didn't need, making them $3,200. They were lucky that Abigail's parents gave them a $4,500 wedding gift. In total, they were able to borrow $10,000 from their parents, without an obligation to pay back. These were the first major steps. And then, something happened that Abigail had not considered possible—she found a way to increase her income.

She always loved to read and write, so she started to write for websites. She could break up the writing process for a website in short periods of time, and she could write whenever she felt able to do it. It was a perfect fit for her energy level, and it was a major boost for her income. With their increased income and their determined focus to change their circumstances, the remaining debt was paid back in two years. They are very happy together, without debt and without all its associated worries.

The term "empowerment" is used in many different ways. My explanation of empowerment is, finding and increasing your inner strength and your own capacities. Every person has experiences, talents and wishes. In addition, everyone has the opportunity to make choices in daily life. Making choices affects your future. Be willing to take responsibility for your own life and make an effort to discover your strengths and develop your capacities. If you are able to better use your strengths and further develop your capacities, you are engaging in empowerment. This process takes place in your mind. All choices you make are affected by your mind or gut feeling. Your gut feelings originate from your subconscious thinking. By consciously directing your thoughts, you control your subconscious thinking. Making decisions is the foundation to developing your strength and using your capacities in a better way. In other words, empowerment is a form of self-direction.

The Foundation for Empowerment

The foundation for empowerment is self-perception. This is having faith and confidence in your own abilities and in your ability to affect your own life in your own environment. In addition to self-perception, a level of situational awareness is indispensable; you must have insight into your own social environment and develop skills within your social environment. You have influence on your verbal and non-verbal communication. The way your environment reacts with you largely depends on your action. You are in control. Don't try to turn an empowerment switch in your mind; that's simply not possible. What's important is taking the first step. Start with small steps and learn the effect of every single action you take. Reward yourself for every step you take. By rewarding yourself, your steps will increase in pace and size. Rewarding yourself can be as easy as giving yourself a compliment.

Take responsibility for your own future. If you are empowered, you gain more grip on events in your life. You decide what happens. Use your capacities to influence and direct both yourself and your environment. Put your mind to work to direct yourself to the desired future. Influence your own behavior and with that, the behavior of your environment. To make your head go in a certain direction, visualization is a great tool. Imagine what your future looks like, what strengths and capacities you will develop further. Visualize this and try to involve as many senses as possible. If you think visualization is hard, try to imagine the car of your dreams. Chances are that you see an image of your dream car. Congratulations, you have just started visualizing.

Discover Your Strength

The journey of discovery into your own strength is different for everyone. For some people, it is an event during which they suddenly notice they are very good at something. This is a small group. Many people are not aware of their strengths, simply because they have never been confronted with them. In this journey of discovery, people realize in hindsight, once they are very advanced in the process, that they have a certain strength. They can handle more than they initially thought. Their environment plays an important role in this. People who go from passion to their strength have more than once gone through an extremely rough time. When you are going through a rough time, you need to stick with your passion to overcome it. Living for a passion is common among top athletes and artists, and 98% of all people are not top athletes or artists. That doesn't mean you don't have passion. You need to be able and willing to go to extremes for yourself to discover your passion or your strength. The only thing the people around you can do is encourage you; true strength comes from within. At the same time, don't be too hard on yourself. A study from 2011 of the University of Massachusetts shows that no less than two-thirds of all people don't or hardly find their strength of passion. Causes can be found in the environment, fears, insecurities, and living in survival mode.

Use Your Capacities

Everyone is born with strengths and capacities. The challenge lies in discovering your capacities. Not everyone recognizes their own strengths. When something comes easy to you, you don't pay a lot of attention to it and think, "Everyone can do what I can do." People walk on mountains and trip over molehills, indicating how easy it is to overlook your own capacities. If you have trouble identifying your capacities, it is time to get out of your comfort zone and to ask other people. The people around you don't see you the way you see yourself. Others see qualities in you that you take for granted. By asking others, you make yourself vulnerable. It starts with discovering your own capacities. The next step is to see how you can best use your capacities. This is a combination of things you like and things you are good at. The crucial question that remains is, are you doing what you're good at? Do you like what you're doing?

Everyone has capacities for making money. I'll assume you have mapped your capacities. Let's say you work at an insurance office, because you feel you're good at it, but in the evenings and weekends, you spend all your time fixing old cars because it's fun and because you can lose yourself entirely in it. Your income at the insurance office is not great. When asking around, you find out that everyone loves how much you know of these old cars and how amazingly you restore them. It is time to check whether it would be possible to get a better income by starting your own business fixing old cars. As an entrepreneur, you might be able to make more money while putting in the same amount of hours at your current job. In addition to fixing cars, you can come up with a second way to make money with your knowledge of these old cars. You can teach courses, give lectures, start a second garage, start an online business that has no limit, and you could even write a book. How large is your financial capacity? What options do you have to make money? Be creative in expanding your financial capacity. There are more possibilities than you think.

Break Barriers

To increase your financial capacity, you need to break through barriers and get outside of your comfort zone. Everyone is comfortable in their comfort zone, but at the same time, all the great and fun things happen outside your comfort zone. Have the guts to break barriers and to get out of your comfort zone. You will start looking for new ways to make money with things you truly like and are good at. The first step is to explore. In doing so, you can eliminate any uncertainties. Ask yourself, "What's the worst that can happen if you do this?" Visualize your greatest nightmare and name all fears you encounter.

If your actions do involve risks, think of how you will deal with these risks in advance. There are four options in this: acceptance, control, avoidance or insurance.

1. **Acceptance**: If you recognize a risk, know what the impact will be when it happens. You have a choice to accept the risk or not. If you can handle the consequences of the risk happening, this is an option for how to deal with it. For example, if you buy a second-hand fridge, there is a risk that it won't last as long as you want. You can accept this risk and buy another one if it breaks down. You have to be able to buy another fridge; otherwise, you can't bear the risk.

2. **Control**: If you notice a risk, you can try to control it and take the necessary actions to prevent the risk from happening. Let's say the entrance to your garage is very small. There is a risk that you will hit the wall with your beautiful car and scratch it. You can affix foam to the entrance of your garage at the height your car might hit the wall. In this way, you controlled the risk of damaging your car.

3. **Avoidance**: The third option is to avoid the risk. If breaking your leg will influence your life dramatically, don't go on holiday in the mountains skiing. You avoid the risk of breaking your leg by not going on the ski trip.

4. **Insurance**: The last option is to insure the risk. You can buy insurance for everything you think is risky. One of the most well-known risk insurances is your health insurance. If you have a health insurance that covers (almost) all medical expenses, you don't worry that much about your health expenses. The insurance company will pay. The question is, do you want to pay the insurance company or not?

Once you have explored and mapped everything, you could take a leap. However, it would probably be better to take small steps. Small steps make it easier to adjust course. Visualizing your road to the end goal is an important tool in this. Do it, because an idea without action is nothing more than a dream. How can you motivate yourself to keep going? This is an intrinsic motivation. The most important thing is to make it fun. It's not only about achieving the end goal; it is also about the road towards it. Celebrate your milestones and your successes. This is great for your confidence and perseverance.

NLP Techniques for Reducing Stress and Finding Empowerment

Neuro linguistic programming (NLP) is a way to reduce or even eliminate stress and worry. NLP was developed by John Grinder in California in the seventies. According to Grinder, there is a connection between neurological processes, language, and behavioral patterns that is learned through programming. Your neuro pathways can be changed to achieve specific goals in life.

It is not my intention to explain and substantiate all NLP theories. I want to bring four simple NLP techniques to your attention. Everyone who worries or has stress can benefit from learning these simple NLP techniques. Certain techniques can be applied when you are suddenly stressed or unhappy. Other techniques are focused more in the future.

Just like Moneyfulness, NLP cannot prevent you from feeling stressed or unhappy; it simply helps you cope and work toward eliminating that stress. Applying NLP techniques equals taking control of your stress and feeling empowered.

Because you are continuously making decisions, it is useful to test these techniques. Start with something small and insignificant, so that, should something go wrong, it won't be a disaster.

Black-and-White Rewind Technique

If you have unpleasant experiences from the past you still worry about, or if you constantly come up with disaster scenarios for the future, the black-and-white rewind technique can help. It helps you neutralize the negative images from the past and break the link between an emotional vibe and the images. For your future images, this works similarly, since you visualize the negative scenario.

It starts with the past. Something unpleasant has happened, and you are wasting time worrying about this event from the past. For instance, three months ago, you lost your job, and with that, your income. The way this happened was unpleasant, and the gap in your income didn't make it any better. The goal is to be able to think about your dismissal without allowing it to make you emotional.

The first step is to realize that your day of dismissal has passed. I use the dismissal as an example, but you can change it to any unpleasant event from the past. There is a moment in which you decide that it is over, and that you continue to live your life. The moment can be in the past if you have already decided when your unpleasant period was done, but it may also be in the future if you visualize your new job. There is a moment you picture in your mind on which the decision was made about when your unpleasant period was done. Freeze this frame and make it black and white. Think about an old television from before color TV. As soon as you have visualized this image, play some exaggerated circus music with it, or any other tune you consider to be silly. You have an end frame and a start frame. The end frame is with a new job and income, and the start frame is from the time with your old job and income. You will rewind all events, supported by the circus music, from the end to the beginning. You see everything unfold backwards: people walk backwards, people talk backwards (visualize how weird this would sound), your coffee cup fills itself up, etc. You end with an image from the beginning, when you were still enjoying your previous job and did not anticipate any problems. The second time, you rewind the movie from the end to the beginning, but this time accelerated. This leads to a sort of Charlie Chaplin slapstick movie in rewind. Details are not important; the story and the experience are what count. Try to recreate the negative feeling of your dismissal day. You will notice that your emotion is much less intense than it was before you started this exercise. Keep rewinding your movie, accelerated, with music, until you feel like your emotion has been neutralized. Usually, this is somewhere between two and five times.

Imagine yourself on a massive movie screen, looking extremely relaxed. Fast forward your movie, in color and in way in which you see yourself do the right things and hear yourself say the right things. Instead of the disaster scenario, you see an image in which everything goes perfectly, the way you want it. You respond to everything in a relaxed and calm manner. Try to retrieve that old unpleasant feeling that you had with a certain situation before you did this exercise. See yourself staying calm, and in the future situation, see yourself addressing the situation in a state of relaxation.

This is a great technique to apply to your inhibiting convictions, especially if you have a hard time converting your inhibiting convictions into the positive. Your conviction is stuck in your mind. There's a statement or event of which you think that might happen and you want to change the feeling associated with it into a positive conviction. The black-and-white rewind technique makes you take your inhibiting conviction and come up with a disaster scenario, how you respond to it and cope with it. Rewind your movie in black and white, with silly music. Now, take your new conviction in color and play it forward. Your negative feelings with your old conviction have been neutralized and your good feeling about your new conviction has taken its place.

Feeling Reversal Technique

You have an acute negative and unpleasant feeling and you want to get rid of it, you must reverse the feeling. This technique is used reactively when you detect that you're having an unpleasant or negative feeling or another feeling you would like to get rid of, such as anger, rage, fear or panic. It starts with becoming aware of the fact that you're not feeling good and deciding that it's time to stop that.

You're worrying about how to make it to the end of the month without money in the bank. You feel terrible about this situation, and the acute feeling when you see your bank balance is stress. Your brain keeps going over and over it again, and all kinds of scenarios pass review. Imagine a large STOP sign, as soon as you experience the unpleasant, negative feeling. Assume an attitude in which you have little tolerance for negative feelings, emotions and stress and want to get rid of them quickly. Localize where the negative feeling is in your body. If you're unable to find that place in your body, trust your intuition and take a guess. Observe the feeling. Where is it, where does it start and how does it move? Feelings always move, even if just a bit. When something is not moving, the body won't feel it. Take people who wear lenses, for instance. The first couple of days/weeks, it is like you constantly have a fly in your eye. Your lens, however, doesn't move. After getting used to it, you won't feel your lens anymore.

The unpleasant feeling can move left, right, from top to bottom or vice versa, or it can be a pinching sensation from the outside inwards or a bloated feeling from the inside outwards, or a weight in your stomach pressing down. Where is the feeling and how does it move?

Visualize a white sheet of paper. Follow your intuition to give the unpleasant feeling, such as stress for not having any money in the bank, a color. It doesn't matter what color, as long as it isn't white. Draw or paint the feeling on the white sheet using a crayon or pencil, using the color of your emotion. Discover the pattern of the motion. Does it rotate? Picture the pattern of the motion in your body in the color you have given it.

The next step is to, again, based on your intuition, take a color that makes you feel good. Take a color that makes you feel relaxed and calm. Draw the opposite pattern of stress with a positive color. Imagine that your dark brown negative color moves upward. Take your positive color, maybe its yellow, and draw from top to bottom from your throat to your abdomen. The entire negative pattern is replaced by a positive color that moves in the opposite direction. When both colors mix, go back and observe the location and motion again.

Take the sheet in front of you, with your positive color, and allow the feelings that color evokes to fill you up. Literally press the sheet against your body to help you visualize that feeling. Take your positive color into your body and make the opposite motion of the negative feeling. If the negative feeling pushes inward from the outside, your positive color will push outward from the inside. Keep repeating this motion and then accelerate. Do this until you can feel the negative feeling subside, to the point that it may even disappear.

Subsequently, send your brain in the right direction. Take a moment from the past during which you felt great. Build a library of good or happy moments when you felt good. You are central in this good moment. Experience what it was like, how good it felt. When you still had a great buffer in your savings account or when you still had your job. Memories will bring back this good feeling. Where does the good feeling begin and how does it move? Keep repeating this pattern and pace it up (while slowing down some of them). Keep repeating this pattern so you'll feel good for the rest of the day.

Sexy Voice and Exaggeration

Everyone has negative thoughts. Your negative spiral is complete when you start to panic about those thoughts. Everything you give attention grows, including panic. Send your brain in a different direction, away from your negative thoughts. Fighting it or resisting it will not work; you will only consume a lot of time thinking that you shouldn't think about it. What should you do then? There are two options, both with the same effect.

To practice, think about a negative thought, one that invokes negative feelings by simply thinking about it. An example thought or conviction might be, "I am bad with money." Let this negative thought pass review a couple of times and you'll notice that this thought has a certain sound. Usually, this is an unpleasant and grumpy sound. Repeat the thought a couple of times, and after a while, you are the one deliberately invoking the thought, which gives you control. You will then gradually change the sound of your voice. Change the unpleasant, negative voice in your head into the sexiest voice you can imagine. Repeat your negative thought a couple of times with your slow and sexy voice. By repeating it with your sexy voice, your brain will respond. Your brain will consider your negative thought or conviction to be silly. And just like that, your negative thought or inhibiting conviction no longer is a truth in your brain.

The second way to neutralize negative thoughts is by exaggeration. Use the same negative conviction, "I am bad with money." Imagine that you are so bad with money that your conditions are worse than the poorest people on the planet. Imagine that your circumstances are worse than those who have survived natural disasters.

Your brain will develop a counter response. It will say, "Stop right there. You're taking this too far. My situation isn't that bad." It will help you neutralize your stress and maybe even practice a little gratitude for what you do have.

A Happier Life

By empowering yourself and by making full use of your personal and financial capacity, you'll lead a happier life. Leading a happy life is something everyone wants. If you don't want to be happy, I recommend finding other trainings and seeking help. Everyone is entitled to a happy life. You have to shape it yourself and make daily efforts for it. Go for long-term happiness and not for short-term happiness. Short-term happiness is found in addictions and pleasures that give you short-lived joy. Long-term happiness is promoted by having enough capital.

The marshmallow experiment in children shows that very early on in life, it can be predicted whether a child will be able to postpone their needs for a greater good. Is the child impulsive? If so, it will choose short-term happiness over long-term happiness. Or, is the child able to leave that single marshmallow alone, so he will have another one, effectively doubling his candy.

The experiment showed that children who are able to control their impulses, and postpone their needs, are more successful in life than children who are not able to wait and who go for short-term happiness. Being able to postpone giving in to temptation and fast profit and fast pleasure leads to a successful life. This characteristic shows whether you are able to persevere for large profits and more stable happiness.

Boost Your Energy

Have you ever experienced it—the feeling of being in a flow? You are working on something and you lose all sense of time or ego. This can be at any time. For instance, when you are making music, exercising, submersed in work or in someone else that consumes you.

Configure your life in such a way that you reach this flow more often. It will make you more positive, successful and happier.

The first step is sleep. Do you recognize the feeling in the morning after a good night sleep? This will not happen after one night of good sleep; it will happen if you sleep enough hours a night for a longer period in time. If you have trouble falling asleep, try meditation when you're lying in bed.

Another energy boost is healthy food. If you adjust your eating routines to healthier food, you will probably lose weight as well. This all adds up to a more energetic life. If you want to speed up the process of losing weight, you should also start exercising (if you haven't exercised for some time, find a specialist to help you get started). It doesn't really matter what exercises you are going to do, as long as you like what you do. There are many more ways to gain energy and get yourself into a flow state more readily, but these are the basics. Don't do these and you'll be facing an uphill battle.

Look for Role Models

Your immediate environment consists of about 10 people. These are the people closest to you; they are the ones you talk to most. These can be people from work or hobbies or people from your private life. How do these people approach life? Are they empowered and do they use all capacities? Or, are they people who are continuously complaining and looking for negative attention. Are they energetic people with a positive attitude, or are they the opposite?

Try to find out how much these people make. The theory is, you make about the average of what these 10 people around you make. Are they people who can inspire you to go higher in life, or are they people who are pulling you down? If you change (part of) your life, will these people still fit in your future plans? Be aware of who you deal with. I'm not asking you to judge them, only to make clear choices. There's nothing wrong with pulling someone up; in fact, it is a good thing, as long as this person wants to be pulled up, if it makes them happy.

A role model is a person or personality who serves as an example for a certain group of people. These can be actors, political leaders and other heroes. You can find them close to home in your local environment, everyone can be a role model. A lot of people see their father or mother as a role model, especially in the beginning, because you spend a lot of time with them. This explains why so many people follow in the footsteps of their parents. Choose your own role model. Choose someone who stands out to you without bearing a role model stamp or label. A role model is someone who consistently adds value for you. They are people who help, inspire and support you in your ideas. Just be yourself. That is why everyone can be a role model; this is what the strength of a role model is. You may be a role model to someone else without even knowing it. Someone can temporarily serve as a role model. As soon as you have learned to do what you value in your role model, it is time to raise the bar and to find a new role model.

Stop Complaining

Empowerment and complaining are arch enemies. Complaining is a bad habit, and it makes you extremely unhappy. In fact, according to studies, it truly can be a fatal behavior. Time to stop complaining and extend your lifespan. The extra joy in life has not yet been specified. According to studies by Duke University Carolina about brain activity, negative thoughts can alter your brain. The more often a negative thought repeats itself, the more solid the negative connection in your brain. By complaining, you repeat information, and by repeating, you better memorize information.

Be aware of your own complaints, including your money complaints. If you want to stop, ask your partner, a colleague or friend to alert you when you're complaining. By making others alert you, you'll truly be confronted with it, and you can learn from it. Proactive solutions are another possibility. Let's say your partner buys the groceries but always forgets something. Your habit is to complain about it towards your partner. Next time, proactively make a grocery list to help your partner not forget. The thing you complained about will turn out to be a futility. Rationalize your complaining behavior and accept reality. Don't worry about it too much. You'll live a longer and healthier life if you don't stress and complain.

Keep Learning

Learning is always good for you; it makes you a better person. You can learn in many different ways. The classic way of learning is from reading a book. A variant of reading books is watching videos online. It is easier, faster and gives you the information you need. The only downside is that this information doesn't stick as well as when you read and summarize. Another frequently used way to learn is to experience something. Do new things and learn from them. That is why experiential experts are valued so much. They tell their story based on their own experience. You can learn a lot from a role model. Copying behavior and the attitude of your role model makes you learn. At a certain point, you're no longer copying your role model, but you have given it your own twist. The last important way of learning is to attend training and courses, both online and live.

Do you want to be stronger in life financially? It is necessary to learn about financial matters. Managing your money and making it grow makes you stronger. You'll feel better if you have a solid financial foundation. What you learn about financial matters has an effect on the direction you'll be investing in. In the chapter "Assets," I will discuss this to more detail. If you are planning on investing in stock, you need to learn how the stock market works, what to look for and how to invest. Crowdfunding is a similar method of investing but with a higher sense of insecurity. Are you interested in real estate? Conduct local research into the real estate market and explore all laws and regulations to discover the pitfalls. Learn about your investments. Attend training, read books and follow webinars. A lot of information can be found online, but don't forget to ask around in your own circle. Others can often help you get started, and people generally like it when you ask them these things. By asking them, you show them that you value them.

A Money Exercise

Investing in the stock market is one of the best ways to put your money to use for you. But, the stock market is complicated to understand at first. You need to spend time observing it and learning about it before jumping in with two feet. So, as you read this book and start to get your own finances in better shape, I want you to learn everything you can about the stock market. That way, when you're ready, you can get started right away.

Here's how to do it. Pretend you have $10,000 of Monopoly money, or fake money that you will "invest" in shares. Select a group of three companies in the same sector, those that have similar products or services, and analyze them over the next month or two. Choose a sector you understand pretty well; that way, when things fluctuate, you'll be better prepared to know what caused those fluctuations. Look at their most recent annual statements and compare them. Get familiar with the financial language and reports inside. Look out for any news regarding any of these companies. Most of all, check in every day to see how your $10,000 of Monopoly money is growing or shrinking.

Is one company doing better than the others? What happens when you allocate more of your money to it over the others? At what point do you feel like it's too risky to put all your money in one company?

The purpose of this exercise is to practice, practice, practice. Get comfortable now so that you can make your money work for you later.

Are you in control of your money, or is your money in control of you? The rat race continues with or without you. How do your surroundings affect you? How much money do you have to spend on certain affairs? You decide what you pay, not only in terms of money but also in terms of freedom and time. Find out what your drives are for making money, why and how you spend it. Your mindset regarding money is extremely important. In various countries, burning money is forbidden; you can even go to jail for it. That is how powerful and important money is, even though it is nothing more than a piece of paper about which agreements have been made. Imagine the power of giving. Bill and Melinda Gates give away massive amounts of money. The amount itself is not important; the act of giving is what's important. The bigger the amount, the more you can do with it, that much is clear. Those who give more than they take will be more successful in time. Money allows you to realize things, including poverty reduction, which is something Moneyfulness contributes to. Your contribution helps eliminate poverty. You can give in countless of ways, and you can make our world a wonderful place by giving.

Summary Empowerment

- Empowerment is a form of self-direction and originates in your mind.
- What capacities do you have?
- Discover your own financial capacity.
- Break barriers and stop complaining.
- Get in the flow and stay there.
- Find a role model or multiple role models for various areas.
- Keep learning, not only about financial matters.
- Do the money exercise.
- Be aware of the power of money in the positive sense.
- Use the special techniques to neutralize stress towards the past, the present or the future.
- Make the right decisions.

The next chapter is about you. Moneyfulness is about you and how you deal with the concept of money. You'll learn several special techniques to calm yourself.

Chapter 7
Y–YOURSELF

"The strength of your personal financial resources is
equivalent to the quality of your financial decision-making."
—**Wayne Chirisa**

D o you hear voices in your head? I do, and they can have entire
discussions, come up with disaster scenarios and come up with
solutions. In itself, there's nothing wrong with this crowd in
your mind, as long as they don't dominate. The voices in your head are
your consciousness.

Let's say you have an inhibiting conviction, such as "money is the
root of all evil." In this conviction, you have a strong negative feeling.
You are convinced of the fact that having money is very bad and that
money only leads to bad things. Say the following conviction out loud
every day: "Money is good, I am happy with every amount that I receive,
and money allows me to do good things." Do this for several weeks, and
then read your inhibiting conviction again. The negative feeling with

this claim will have disappeared. You may even start feeling good about having money. This is only an example that you can use at your own discretion.

Everyone is different, which is why we dislike labels. But sometimes identifying with certain characteristics can help you recognize certain truths about yourself. I have created eight archetypes based on common reactions toward money that I have seen. Based on these different characterizations, you can find out what your money talent is and what your money challenge is. The eight archetypes are based on eight sacred money archetypes.[3] Find the type that suits you best. If you know what type suits you best, you can focus on your money talent and your money challenge. It is about the awareness concerning your talent and challenges.

The 8 Sacred Money Archetypes

I will walk you through all eight types. First, I'll give you a brief description of the type, followed by the associated talent and challenge.

Controller

The controller uses money as a way to measure his success. Everything the controller achieves can be measured by money. Controllers can achieve great things in the world and have great impact. The inner being of the controller is driven by fear. The good news is, they are unstoppable. The bad news is, they are unstoppable.

Talent: Building a company in which everyone can thrive. Innovating and discovering new opportunities for growth. Being decisive and creating value.

Pitfall: Not being able to enjoy living in the moment. Being unrealistic about how much it costs to retire. The feeling of never having enough money.

---

3   http://sacredmoneyarchetypes.com/

Romantic

The romantic likes making the most of their life. They love the good things in life. They spoil themselves and others. The romantic is very generous. They lead a lavish lifestyle in which money flows abundantly and with debt lurking around the corner. They are impulse buyers because it feels good to treat themselves and others, without thinking about financial consequences.

Talent: Believing there will always be more. Being generous to others. Supporting the economy.

Pitfall: Lavish lifestyle. Avoiding everything that has to do with money. Buying first, feeling guilty later.

Alchemist

The alchemist is a fascinating type. They have a love/hate relationship with money. They have strong emotions tied to money. If they can organize their energy, have focus and attention to convert their ideas into financial success, they get exactly what they want. They can inspire entire populations in a powerful manner and make a lot of money doing so. Their focus is on the creation of money, not on selling, and on helping people in ways they are willing to pay for. If they focus on this, they will be able to improve the world.

Talent: Creating ideals, valuing others, thinking in possibilities and opportunities.

Pitfall: Financial dependence. Not creating any financial goals and habits. Discarding money and considering it as a negative catalyst for change.

Collector

The collector has a strong connection with money and values and respects money. The motivation for a collector is a deeply rooted fear of becoming poor or even worse, going bankrupt. The collector lacks faith.

The problem with the collector is that he falls into his own pitfall; these are limits he has come up with himself. The best place to be as a collector is where you allow yourself a sense of expansion. Come out of the "I'll do it myself" mode and start trusting others and spending money.

Talent: Good at saving. Creates financial independence. Has financial responsibility.

Pitfall: Stinginess and lack of generosity. Feeling guilty about expenses and doubting investments.

Caretakers

Caretakers have a hard time defining their boundaries. They easily give away all their possessions, in particular to family or others they care about. Others take advantage of their need to save others. If, as a caretaker, you are aware of the fact that this is your pitfall, and if you set clear boundaries with regard to money, you indicate that you value the other.

Talent: Loyal, generous. Provide great added value.

Pitfall: Wanting to save others, to the point of martyrdom. Feeling hateful or guilty. Ignoring your own needs for the benefit of someone else's.

Connecter

Everything is about relationships and people, people, and more people. The connecter naturally has no relationship with money; it truly is not important. They deal with money as if it is a routine, with a checklist. The relationship with money has to be taught and dictated to them. The connector has huge faith and optimism and a lot of confidence in money. They don't need to keep up with others in the world. Money as status means nothing to them. The connecter can perceive a large sense of peace. Others can disadvantage the connector in the financial field because they have so little interest in money.

Talent: Does not get stressed. Great confidence and optimism. Doesn't compare himself to others, particularly not financially.

Pitfall: Lack of financial independence. Money doesn't make you stronger. You are overwhelming, based on debt.

Celebrity

The celebrity likes showing they have money. They buy expensive cars, beautiful jewelry and large houses. The celebrity can have a lot of status symbols that are important. Celebrities are charismatic. Because of the expensive lifestyle of the celebrity, they can get in significant debt; they love spending money. If they are aware of their expense pattern, they can avoid debt.

Talent: Leadership. Helping others to make a great impression. Developing a luxurious paradigm so that others can improve themselves based on that.

Pitfall: Compulsive spending. Spending money to avoid feelings. Feeling empty and being criticized.

Outsider

The outsider loves money and is fascinated by it. He likes to take large financial risks. Money and simplicity are not appealing to the outsider. They love adrenaline, are very competitive and love to win. Financial complexity is no problem to them. They go against the stream anyway and do things their own way. There is a great focus on money. That doesn't mean they don't have any debt; they are not collectors, and they keep track of all figures. The outsider is someone who will sell you something for more money, knowing that he can get it for less somewhere else. They collect the higher money, only to get the product cheaper elsewhere, and deliver it in accordance with the agreement. They like trading; it is exhilarating for them.

Talent: Structured negotiations and cutting deals with financial complexity. Focus on figures and financial details. Taking risks.

Pitfall: Taking risks with the opportunity of losing a lot. Creating great financial profit, but losses as well. The willingness to gamble with financial security.

Which Type Are You?

Take a good look at yourself and think about what type suits you best to be able to avoid your challenges. Dealing with your challenges means controlling your deepest wishes. This requires discipline and willpower. You have the urge to head in a certain, less smart direction with money. Ignore this urge and head in the right direction. This won't be easy, especially in the beginning. It feels like you have to give up a piece of who you are. This is your challenge, not someone else's. Take your talent for money and financial affairs. Compare these to your current way of life. Apply this consciously, and you will grow stronger. The best thing is, you discover a strong side of yourself that you haven't developed yet. You have probably never been aware of it, because it is so easy for you.

Who You Truly Are

The outside of your head is the physical, visible side of your head. The inside of your head is subdivided into three compartments. It's not like you can actually point out these three compartments; they are present throughout your head. In your head, there's the mental part, which includes your rational thoughts. Your rational thoughts are based on learned knowledge and experiences from the past. The outside of your head doesn't show what you perceive as rational and irrational. The second compartment in your brain is the emotional part. As long as you are able to keep a straight face, nobody will notice something with regard to your emotions. An artificial version of this is a Botox treatment. People who have received an excessive amount of Botox in their face, come across as emotionless. There are people who love showing emotions and there are also plenty of people who don't. Whether or not you want to show emotions is a rational thought. The third compartment in your brain is the spiritual part. The spiritual part of your thoughts in your head doesn't reveal itself in a lot of people. People are ashamed of their spiritual thoughts, because they don't want to be considered abnormal.

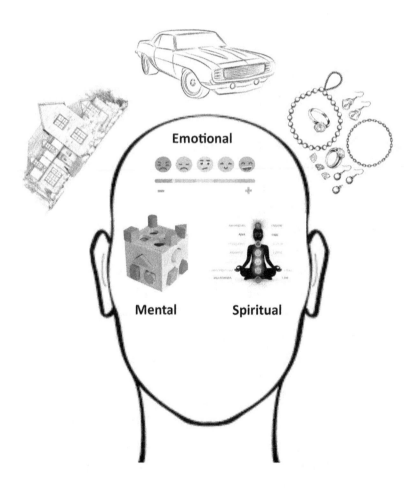

10 Steps to Realize What You Want

In the chapter "Opportunities," you saw that setting goals is important. To actually realize what you want, setting goals is your first big step. First, you need to know what you want and why you want it. I will walk you through the steps from dream to realization, one by one.

1. Set clear goals. If you can't envision them clearly, reread the chapter about opportunities.
2. Visualize your goals and the end result. What does it feel like to achieve your goal? Try to feel what it would be like to have realized your goal. Use as many of your five senses as possible when visualizing (feeling, seeing, hearing, smelling and tasting).
3. Implement. Everything depends on taking your first step towards your goal. Keep taking steps to get closer to your goal. You don't have to have a fully detailed roadmap in advance to be able to take your first steps towards the goal. In fact, changes and setbacks will cause you to take detours that will eventually lead to your goal.
4. Clearly visualize the results of your actions. All steps you take will lead to a result. If a step does not lead to the right or correct result, immediately correct it in your next action.
5. Show commitment, don't be distracted or tempted. Don't be distracted by non-essential issues. Showing commitment is related to overcoming fears and getting outside your comfort zone. Do things you have never done before. Don't be tempted by the enemy called laziness.
6. Your choices determine your success. Every choice you make to do something is always a good choice. Doing nothing is worse than doing something wrong. If you do nothing, nothing will ever happen. The more mistakes you make, the sooner you will find the right path.

7. Nothing is impossible; there is no can't. Your brain is a marvelous idea machine. Put your conscious and subconscious brain to work creatively; 99 percent of all people work on achieving realistic goals. That is where you'll find your competition. How about setting unrealistic goals.

8. Be willing to work harder than the rest. Being willing to work harder, doesn't mean being willing to work more than the rest. Come up with smart strategies to reach your goal faster and easier. Your brain is working harder.

9. Find the right people. Find role models for specific goals. Hang out with role models who have already achieved your envisioned goal.

10. Be willing to keep learning (and from the right people). Always keep learning. You can do so in various ways, from books, courses, role models, etc.

Making Good Decisions

To avoid problems in your future, you need to make the right decisions today. NLP can also help you make better decisions. Consciously or subconsciously, you can sense the quality of your decisions. Imagine yourself in a shoe store, fitting a pair of shoes that don't fit and are the wrong color. You are in the store, and deep down, you know you will never wear the shoes that don't fit well and don't have the perfect color. You are almost out of money, the month is far from over, but still, you buy the shoes that don't fit well and don't have the perfect color. You can save a lot of money by listening to your gut feeling. Your subconscious knows in advance whether a decision is good or bad.

Begin observing how your brain deals with good and bad decisions. The quality of your decisions is reflected in your three main senses: how you see, feel or hear something. To find out how your brain makes good and bad decisions, you need to think about a bad buy you once had.

The pair of shoes that didn't fit and that had the wrong color. You can visualize the bad buy to test how your brain makes the selection. The brain tends to place images in a space around you. The image has a place, not where your bad buy is physically located, but the image of the bad buy that you're currently visualizing. For most people, this is left or right (sometimes high or low). As soon as you have found the place, you look at what color it is associated with, what negative feeling it invokes and what thoughts it invokes.

Visualize a buy that immediately made you happy and has only given you positive memories. This image has a different color, a positive emotion and a pleasant thought. This image is located elsewhere than the previous, negative image you visualized. If the negative image is left, chances are, the positive image is right.

Both images, positive and negative, are located elsewhere. Observe what different feelings you experience with the images and note the difference in thoughts. It is important to note the differences in images and colors that invoke different feelings and thoughts before you actually make a decision.

To try out the decision-making process, imagine something small you need to make a decision about, such as a pair of shoes or something like that. Whether you buy the shoes or not will not have major consequences for the rest of your life. Start small to practice and gradually move towards bigger decisions.

In this example, I will assume that your good decisions are right and bad decisions left. You make your sample decision, the pair of shoes, and work with this. You visualize buying the pair of shoes as an extremely good decision. Then, you will think about the image to see where it appears and whether all associated feelings and thoughts belong there. The image as a whole must be a correct image, with feeling and thoughts. If the entire image ends up on your right, it is a good decision. If the purchase of the pair of shoes ends up on your left with the bad decisions, this doesn't mean that you shouldn't buy shoes at all, just not this pair. If your decision ends up with the bad decision, you can adjust something, shape it differently or approach the same situation in a different manner. You could ask for shoes in a different color, for instance; perhaps they might even be a better fit. If you have adjusted your decision, do the exercise again. If your decision appears on your right, it has become a good decision. You can try moving the image to the left to see whether it secretly isn't a bad decision after all. In case of doubt about your decision, moving it is a useful extra option. Between both image moments, it is useful to think about something else for a second, such as your vacation or a hobby. As long as the image keeps popping up on your right, you need to carry out the decision as quickly and as well as possible. If the image remains on your left, it's time to forget about it and to continue with the rest of your life. Your new result is the final result. Your subconscious has evaluated everything again and has reached the final conclusion.

By making the right decisions, you can avoid bad buys. By avoiding bad buys, you can realize a higher bank balance. Where you used to pay for impulse purchases, you now keep your wallet in your pocket in case of a bad decision. This way, you can create more room to save and invest, or, in the beginning, to repay your debt.

Congratulations, you have completed the Money Method. In Moneyfulness, the Money Method is the link to mindfulness. In the next chapter, you will go to work practically, in a different manner. You will take a look at your past, with the help of the Hollywood principle.

Summarize Yourself

- There are eight different archetypes with regard to money. What archetype suits you best?
- Make use of your money talent.
- Beware of your money challenge.
- Go through the six stages to change your conviction.
- Take the ten steps to realize what you want.

Chapter 8
HOLLYWOOD PRINCIPLE

You must gain control over your money
or the lack of it will forever control you.
—**Dave Ramsey**

I frequently used to give workshops for entrepreneurs. One of my students was Nicole. Nicole had little knowledge of the financial part of her company. After the workshop, I had a conversation with her. She was a photographer. The financial part just would not click with Nicole. Talking to her about her work as a photographer, we reached the conclusion that a financial statement is comparable to a movie. There's an opening image and a closing image, and the whole story takes place in between those two images. This work method can also be applied to your financial situation.

In the basic sense, every movie is similar. Every movie has an opening shot, a storyline in the middle, and an end shot. But, every movie tells a different story—no two are the same. The same applies to your story—your story is unique. To properly map your story, you can use the "Hollywood principle."

With this principle, you'll take a year from your life and turn it into a movie. Obviously, you need to make the movie interesting. The opening and ending of your movie are beautiful shots, but the story in between forms the entire image. Get familiar with the Hollywood principle based on a well-known movie. One of the biggest and most compelling Hollywood movies of all times is *Titanic*.

People know eight basic emotions[4]:

1. Love
2. Fear
3. Joy
4. Anger
5. Sadness
6. Surprise/amazement
7. Embarrassment
8. Loathing

Titanic

The movie *Titanic* only covers a couple of days out of the lives of fictional characters Rose and Jack, in which these eight basic emotions are amply addressed. Rose is a rich woman who enters the ship, together with her fiancé and her mother. On the outside, everything looks perfect: sailing first-class to America on a ship that could not sink. In the beginning, Rose wants to jump ship because she is being forced into a life she doesn't want. She feels trapped in her golden cage. The cage remains gold when she enters into the "fairytale" courtship with her fiancé. Jack is another passenger aboard the ship. Jack has won passage on the ship

---

4   https://study.com/academy/lesson/robert-plutchiks-wheel-of-emotions-lesson-quiz.html

through a game of poker. He sails third-class. Jack is an artist and takes every day as it comes. Jack has no money, but he feels as if he is the "king of the world."

The Opening Shot of *Titanic*

The movie begins with the image of the faded glory of the Titanic. The Titanic is at the bottom of the ocean. This is a fixed image that can't be changed. The Titanic no longer moves forward or backwards. Very gently, they move through the remains of the Titanic, using an underwater camera. In the present, they look at what was once the end of an exciting story. In the movie, there are a lot of switches between the past and the present, in which Rose tells the story of what happened 84 years ago. Rose takes you back to the moment when she entered the Titanic, when it was still considered an unsinkable ship.

The Story of *Titanic*

With one good hand of poker, the poverty-stricken Jack wins a third-class ticket to America. He is extremely happy, and together with his partner, he needs to run to the Titanic to get on board. Rose makes it appear as if she owns a fortune. Both go aboard the Titanic; Rose sails first-class, Jack third-class. Before long, it becomes apparent that Rose is directed towards a future by her environment, a future she dreads. Fear and anger drive her to the stern of the ship, where she climbs over the railing, planning on jumping into the ice-cold water. That is how oppressive Rose perceives the rich life she leads. Jack goes to the stern of the ship at exactly the right moment. To his surprise, he sees how rich Rose is planning to take her own life. Jack saves her life and is invited by Rose's grumpy fiancé to join them for dinner. After dinner, Rose and Jack go to the third-class deck, where a party is going on as well. Rose's mother reminds her almost daily of the fact that they are almost out of money. By constantly reminding her of this, she wants to force Rose to marry her fiancé. The love between Jack and Rose blooms. Jack draws Rose on a sofa, wearing only the necklace with the big diamond. The Titanic hits a massive iceberg that was hidden under water. One by one, the compartments of the ship are flooded. Rose's fiancé discovers this and wrongly blames Jack for the theft of the necklace. The Titanic cannot be saved; it will sink. There are only lifeboats available for fifty percent of the passengers. Without shame, first-class ladies and children get into the available lifeboats with few others. Eventually, three quarters of all passengers die. Jack does not survive, to the sorrow of Rose, who does survive. Now Rose, at the age of 102, is on the ship that is undertaking the expedition.

The End Shot of *Titanic*

In the end shot of the movie, 102-year-old Rose walks to the stern of the ship. With toenails painted in red, she climbs onto the railing. One hand firmly grasps the railing, and the other is hiding something. It is the necklace with the diamond. This diamond could have brought her a fortune. She held onto this necklace for all these years and never sold it. The precious memories attached to this necklace were of much more value to her. To complete the circle, she throws the necklace into the water. You see the necklace slowly sink to the Titanic. The ship is still on the same location it was 84 years ago. Rose entrusts the necklace with the big diamond to the ocean; she takes it back to the place where it belongs: the Titanic. This beautiful necklace belongs to the sea. The end shot of the movie once again is the sunken Titanic, a fixed, unchangeable image.

The opening shot and the end shot look the same, but there's a huge difference. When Rose enters the boat and sees the Titanic via a camera, the Titanic doesn't include the expensive neckless. The end shot looks nearly the same, only Rose threw the necklace into the ocean to return it to where it belongs. So, the value of the Titanic has increased during the movie with the value of the necklace. It's the same with your assets and debts. The list of assets and debts will not change that much over a year, only the numbers you add to the lines will be different. Therefore, your opening shot and your end shot will look more or less the same, but they can mean very different things.

The Hollywood Principle

We now link the concept of the movie to mapping your situation. This is the Hollywood principle. Every movie has an opening-shot image. If you map the past 12 months, you'll have an opening shot of 12 months ago. The start is mapping all your possessions and debt 12 months ago. The main part of the movie consists of the story itself. Everyone has a story. Take your story of the past 12 months. Everything that happened in the past 12 months is your movie. What income and expenses did you have? The end shot of your movie is also a fixed image; it cannot be changed. Take today as the day to map all your possessions and debt. Now you have your movie of the past 12 months. With the help of the BANK Method, which we will cover in the coming chapters, you can make your own movie of the next 12 months. You are the director of your own movie. Make sure it will be an interesting movie that is fun to watch and amazing to experience. You are in control, so let your imagination run wild. You can make the movie of your future shorter or longer than 12 months at your own discretion. Because you have just practiced with the past 12 months, it might be easier to have your future also span 12 months.

Your Opening Shot

The opening shot is the start point of your movie. Check how much your possessions were worth 12 months ago. This can partly be retrieved; the rest needs to be an estimate. When it is hard to find past amounts, an estimate is fine too. You create an opening shot for your movie. Nobody but you knows what your opening shot looked like. Compare it to the

Titanic. This ship has lived under water for so many years that nobody knows whether everything is accounted for and what it once looked like. The same applies to your memory. Nobody memorizes a detailed image from the past. Your memory has the annoying tendency to present everything more beautifully than it actually was. To help you, I have added a table to this chapter where you can list all possible possessions and debt. If you don't have certain possessions or debt, just leave the field blank. Start filling out this overview as accurately as possible.

Assets

Bank accounts	12 months ago	Today
Current account 1		
Current account 2		
Current account 3		
Savings account 1 (total value)		
Savings account 2 (total value)		
Savings account 3 (total value)		
Other accounts 1 (like e.g. cash or bitcoin)		
Other accounts 2 (like e.g. cash or bitcoin)		
Other accounts 3 (like e.g. cash or bitcoin)		
Total cash in bank accounts		

Investments	12 months ago	Today
Shares		
Bonds		
Funds holding/spreading shares for you		
Real estate that is rented out		
Total investments		

Pensionplan	12 months ago	Today
Pension funds		
Pension insurance funds		
Entrepreneur's pension plan in the company		
Other pension facilities		
Total pensionplan		

Common use objects	12 months ago	Today
Sales value of your owned house		
Second home/beach house not rented out		
Furniture		
ICT equipment		
Other inventory in and around the house		
Sale value of your car(s)		
Boat		
Motorcycle		
Other transportation		
Collections		
Jewels		
Other valuable posessions		
Total common use objects		

Total Assets		

Debts

Name	12 months ago	Today
Mortgage		
Mortgage second house/beach house		
Mortgage on property rented out		
Credit card debt		
Mail order debt		
Loans		
Taxes to pay		
Current account debt		
Other debts 1		
Total Debts		

The Story of Your Movie

The Money Method has changed your attitude towards money. This doesn't mean you don't have to map the past 12 months with your old convictions. Take the moment in which your ship departs. See what enters the ship and what leaves the ship. In other words, what is the income you received on your bank accounts in the past year? The second part of the overview are all expenses. Make sure you clearly map where your income came from and where your expenses went. It is important to first map the past, so you can plan your future. Be honest with yourself in the overview. There's no use making things look better than they are. To help you with this, I made you an overview to fill out. It is a guide (a main layout) you can use to document your expenses. Your income, minus your expenses leads to the balance. Add it all up and see whether you have a surplus or a deficit.

Income

Income	Weekly	Monthly	Annually	Total	Per month
Net salary (including bonusses etc.)					
Net business income					
Allowances					
Pension					
Income from rental property					
Dividends received					
Interest received					
Child support					
Other income 1					
Other income 2					
Other income 3					
Total income					

Expenses

Housing	Weekly	Monthly	Annually	Total	Per month
Mortgage					
Rent					
Gas/water/ electricity					
Telephone					
Cleaning costs					
Repair and maintenance					
Home improvements					
Other housing expenses 1					
Other housing expenses 2					
Other housing expenses 3					
Other housing expenses 4					
Total housing costs					

Regular expenses	Weekly	Monthly	Annually	Total	Per month
Food and beverages					
Insurance					
Clothing and shoes					
Personal care					
Gifts					
Daycare children					
Charity					
Interest on loans/ credit cards, etc.					
Other regular expenses 1					
Other regular expenses 2					
Other regular expenses 3					
Other regular expenses 4					
Total regular expenses					

Transportation	Weekly	Monthly	Annually	Total	Per month
Fuel					
Insurances					
Repair and maintenance					
Taxes					
Parking costs					
Public transportation					
Other trans-portation costs 1					
Other trans-portation costs 2					
Other trans-portation costs 3					
Other trans-portation costs 4					
Total transportation costs					

Fun	Weekly	Monthly	Annually	Total	Per month
Going out for dinner					
Movie/theater/ concert					
Hobbies					
Sports					
Vacations					
Other fun 1					
Other fun 2					
Other fun 3					
Other fun 4					
Total fun					

Education	Weekly	Monthly	Annually	Total	Per month
Books					
Trainings					
Seminars					
Professional literature/ contribution professional org.					
Congresses					
Other education 1					
Other education 2					
Other education 3					
Other education 4					
Total education					

Financial obligations	Weekly	Monthly	Annually	total	per month
Pension plan					
Mortgage payments (excl. interest)					
Loan payments (excl. interest)					
Credit card payments (excl. interest)					
Mail order payments (excl. interest)					
Regular savings (growth of your savings account)					
Investments (regular payments to investment funds)					
Other financial obligations					
Total financial obligations					

Total expenses					

Your End Shot

We will now work on your end shot. This works exactly like making the start shot. By comparing these two overviews, you can easily see the progression. The end shot is today. What is the current value of your possessions and the current value of your debt? By subtracting one from the other, you are presented with your current capital. What are you currently worth in terms of money? Try to make the end shot as realistic as possible. Enhancing your current situation is your ego playing tricks on you. Show courage and be as accurate as possible. Go back to the chart you filled out for your opening shot and fill in your end shot numbers, too.

Make Your Future Movie

Now that you have mapped the past, you can paint a great future image. To realize a great future image, you must first make your own movie. How would you like your movie to look? What emotions would you like to experience? Let your imagination run wild. What will happen in the next 12 months? Don't forget to enjoy your journey between today and your end shot a year from now. The end goal is not the most important, but the road towards it is equally important. Try to make the clearest possible movie of the year to come. Visualize how you will get from today to next year. Imagine what is to happen along the way, and try to experience your movie in an intense way. Stimulate as many senses as possible. Visualize your movie, feel your emotions and hear all sounds. If you can, smell and taste everything. The more realistic the movie is in your mind, the bigger the chance of you realizing it.

The next challenge is to make your movie more interesting. You can influence your movie, and our focus is mainly on income and expenses. You are the one who determines what your income is and what you want to do with it. With your income, you can determine what to spend your money on. Decisions from the past have an effect on your future and are negotiable. This allows you to change your movie. Don't underestimate your own influence. You can only spend your money once.

As we stated earlier, Plutchik's eight basic emotions are joy, trust, fear, surprise, sadness, anticipation, anger, and disgust. Each primary emotion also has a polar opposite:

- Joy is the opposite of sadness.
- Fear is the opposite of anger.

- Anticipation is the opposite of surprise.
- Disgust is the opposite of trust.

In crafting your story, remember that it's okay to feel all eight of these emotions at one point or another. Mistakes and missteps happen. You may take a few risks that don't pay off as you'd hoped. Embrace that this is a process that takes time with trial and error.

There are two ways to increase the money you have to spend: you can increase your income and you can reduce your expenses. Take a critical look at your expenses. What expenses are useful and what expenses simply exist because they are paid automatically? The overview from the Hollywood principle is important right now. If you know where your money goes, you can make conscious decisions on whether to buy something or not. This is your first priority. Making choices is not easy, but deciding where your money goes is essential. By making choices, you decide whether you have more or less money in your wallet at the end of the journey.

Opposite to your expenses is your income. As an entrepreneur, you can increase your rates or work more hours. By increasing your rates, you will receive more money for the same goods or services. Increasing your rates does not affect your workload. It provides extra income and increases your opportunities. If you work with hourly rates or something similar, you can work more hours and increase your income. This is comparable to someone in employment. You can take a job on the side or work overtime. The second option requires extra effort.

Once the upcoming 12 months have been planned, you have an image in mind of everything that is to happen in the next 12 months. This automatically leads to a final image. This will be the end shot of your movie about your future. Make the image complete by making an overview of your possessions and debts in a year. You are free to choose a different period or to make a final image in five years. This

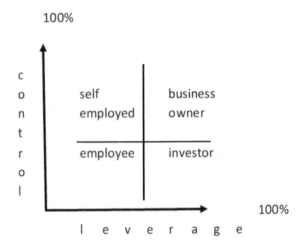

will give you a multi-year planning to work towards. I can imagine that you can't realize all your goals in 12 months. Your image depends on your spending pattern and wishes. The timeframe of achieving an image partly depends on your current situation. If, in the past, you invested part of your buffer in your possessions, achieving the final image may be closer than it is for someone who is currently in debt. If you're in debt, the final image may seem far away, but you can decide what happens.

How to Get There

Your direction has been determined. The next thing to do is to figure out how to get there. This requires some brainstorming. Think of all the ideas you can come up with to save money and to earn more money. The savings will be extracted from the analysis from the past, which you've done before. Have a look at it and delete some costs again.

The other part that requires brainstorming is how to earn more money. There is a limited amount of hours in a day, and you can't work 24/7. So, you have to start to thinking differently. One of the outcomes may be to start your own business. Starting your own business only needs a good idea, nothing else. There are always different routes you can take to realize your ideas. To speed up the process of increasing your income and realizing your ideas, there are four levers you can use. After all, you don't want to do it all by yourself because of your limitation in time.

The Levers

To be able to change your movie and your end image more easily, there are four options to accelerate the process. You will use the levers to achieve more with less effort. For many, this sounds like a fairytale, but with the help of the four options below, it could become reality.

1. **Money:** if you have plans or ideas but no financial means to realize them, consider starting a crowdfunding campaign. Find investors that have faith in your idea and who want to invest in it. To this end, you may have to give up part of your company and control of your company. Look at Facebook for instance. People who have been there since the beginning, and helped Facebook get big, receive a share in Facebook in return, and they are now millionaires.

   There are always people or companies who want to finance good ideas. And yes, they want a piece of the pie. But, do you prefer 50% of a fortune or 100% of nothing? Financers are putting their money to work in your idea. It's your job to make your dream come true using their money.

2. **Time:** Form a team around you. Other people love to work for you. Someone who strongly takes the lead is formed by others. You can hire staff for a fee, but you can also consider offering shares or a fixed turnover percentage during the collaboration period. This can be lucrative to both parties.

3. **Knowledge:** Begin with the network in your immediate surroundings: people you know and trust. They want to help

you, but you have to ask them. Attend a practical training that suits your goal. Find a mentor or coach who wants to help you and reward them with other services you can perform for your mentor or coach.

4. **Systems:** Existing companies have developed systems to promote marketing and sales. If you are still at the beginning, there's a lot you have to invent. Make an inventory of the companies that come before or after you in the process. Work together with these companies and make use of their existing systems. This can be for a fee per sold product, via the already established system.

Include all four of these options in your considerations. See which one suits you best and start with that. All four options are easy to implement. Good luck with your accelerator.

The Four Quadrants of Income

People can be subdivided into four quadrants. You may be present in more than one quadrant. The four quadrants are determined by the level of control you want to have and in which you use the leverage. Someone who is self-employed has a higher level of control about the work to be performed. Hours are exchanged for money. What you spend your hours on is fully under your control. Someone in employment has a lot less control of what he or she needs to do. These two groups usually make little use of the leverage effect.

Joris, for example, was traditionally employed. Outside of the company he worked for, he formed a team of people around him that made his life easier. Joris is a tax consultant. He likes filling out tax returns and hates doing chores in and around the house. One to two months a year, he does the work he likes: filling out tax returns. On the other hand, Joris had little to no chores to do in and around the house. Services are exchanged and the levers are mutually made use of: knowledge and time.

The other two groups make a lot of use of the leverage effect. Business owners have a lot of control: they decide what happens. The company is managed, and all four levers are used. The last group consists of investors, and they can be present in all quadrants. Everyone who has shares, for instance, is an investor. The percentage of people only present in the quadrant "investor" and not in the other quadrants is low. If you are only present in the quadrant of the investor, you don't have to work for a living. If this is your dream, you have work to do, but anyone can make this transition.

The beauty of the Hollywood principle is that it allows you to dream big. By picturing what you would like your financial position to be at the end of one or five years, you can break down the steps you need to take to get there. If your goals are lofty, which I hope they are, your ending shot may show you at the helm of a successful business feeling like the "king of the world."

You can't change the past, like Rose couldn't bring Jack back to life, but you can change the future. Jack's future changed radically on a hand of poker, and both of their lives changed when they fell in love. At the end, Rose had to live her life, making a fresh start after the Titanic sunk. The movie *Titanic* shows us that you mustn't forget about the past. It's up to you to write your own movie, with all ups and downs, all emotions and money coming in and going out. Just like how Rose rewrote her life from rich girl entering the Titanic to anonymous, changing her name when she was rescued.

Summary of the Hollywood Principle

- Recognize the eight basic emotions in the movie *Titanic*
- The effect of the Hollywood principle
- The opening
- The story
- The ending
- Make an overview of your possessions and your debt
- Make the overview of your income and expenses
- The leverage effect
- Makes sure to end up in the right quadrant

With the Hollywood principle, you have mainly looked back at your past and flirted a little bit with the future. With the bank management system, you will give your financial future a practical implementation.

Chapter 9
BANK MANAGEMENT

The amount of money that a person has in his bank account
is not determined by his starting capital but by his knowledge
about money and his ability to manage it properly.
—**Sunday Adelaja**

I n prehistoric times and long after, humanity lived without money. Initially, goods were exchanged. Imagine you just shot a buffalo; that could potentially feed you for six months, but that buffalo will go bad long before that. Now, you need to exchange chunks of buffalo meat against other goods as soon as possible. You need pots, pans, animal hides and the roof of your shack repaired. This isn't very convenient; it never comes at the right time. Just like the buffalo meat, certain goods won't survive the time factor. Bartering has long been customary. As time passed, various interchange means arose, such as shells, salt or pieces of precious metal.

Around the year 750 BC, the first coins were made in China, and more were made decades later in the Western world. In various metals, a stamp was used to create an imprint, so that anyone could see the currency and the value the piece of metal represented. Coins are small, easy to trade and won't rot or get destroyed in any other way. Money was born. It wasn't until the 14th century AD that paper money was accepted as a serious alternative.

In North Italy, the first banks arose in the 14th century. The oldest bank that currently exists is the Monte dei Paschi di Siena, although it required external support to survive. The first bankers were goldsmiths. Each goldsmith required a solid safe for his own supply. Before long, other villagers asked them whether their gold and other valuables could be stored in these big, strong safes. Goldsmith rented various parts of their safes out to the villages, which made some extra money on the side. As time passed, he realized that most people never collected their golden coins, and the receipts he wrote were traded on the market to represent the gold. The goldsmith was smart enough to lend the money from his safe that wasn't collected to others who needed it, and to charge interest. More and more villagers came for a loan. The receipts he wrote were traded mutually. So, why not simply write more receipts and use the gold of the villagers as collateral? Because of all this lending activity, the goldsmith became more of a banker than a craftsman.

He made more and more money. It became evident that he had a lot to spend, and the villagers became suspicious. They suspected the goldsmith of spending the money that they had stored with him and threatened to collect their gold instantly. The goldsmith had to reveal his work method. To his surprise, this didn't cause him any trouble. He opened the safe and showed them that their gold was in the safe, as promised. The villagers who had stored their gold at the goldsmith, demanded part of the profit he made on the money he lent based on their gold. This is how the concept of interest at the bank was born. From this moment on, the goldsmith became a full-fledged banker.

The Value of Money

Gold and silver coins had a value linked directly to the value of the metal. Nowadays, there is no single active silver or gold coin left, not to mention the value of paper money. The paper itself has virtually no value. The value of the special piece of paper is a value people attach to agreements associated with the piece of paper. Countries have a certain gold supply that covers the pieces of paper about which agreements have been made. This system was clear. The government knew approximately how many coins and bills were in circulation and how much gold was in the safe. The coverage percentage was easily calculated. In 1950, the credit card was invented. This was the beginning of the increasing digitization of our money. The number of coins and bills actually exchanged is decreasing rapidly. You pay with plastic. Your bank balance has become a large number of ones and zeroes. You can use an app on your phone to make payments, due to which the plastic could soon very well be a thing of the past.

The value that people attribute to money is based on mutual agreements about money. As long as everyone keeps faith in those agreements, there are no problems.

The Future of Money

Money is currently regulated by the government. Together with the central banks, governments have the power to create money. The digitization of money makes it easier to create and control money. Traditional coins and bills will become less and less common and make way for phones, but for now, the governments and central banks are firmly in control.

Crypto coins are new coins that are on the rise. They are a digital currency that is not tangible. Crypto coins are not covered by gold or something similar. The technology behind them is based on block chain. This technology is fully based on mutual trust. A major advantage is that all mutual transactions can easily be traced. By documenting the mutual digital trust, one can always trace where the money came from and where it went. Various crypto coins are still in their infancy. Time will tell whether these non-government regulated currencies will survive.

This brings us to today. What is the value of money? A lot of money has a gold reserve to back it up, however, that doesn't apply to everyone anymore. Individual Euro countries, for instance, own money, but the Euro as a currency does not have a central gold reserve on which the value is based. The gold reserve of the United States remains the same, whereas the debt ceiling is frequently raised. This means the gold backup becomes lower every time, especially since the rise of the digital era currency and underlying values have been growing apart. Because a large portion of the money traffic is digital, money has become nothing but ones and zeroes. This is one of the reasons why the bitcoin was invented. A bitcoin is a truly digital currency. You can actually touch regular currency, but crypto coins are entirely digital. This brings us to the statement: money has become a trust product.

The Importance of Money Management

There are several reasons to manage money flows, even though they are mainly ones and zeroes. Large amounts of cash money are hard to find nowadays. The time that companies handed out salary bags to employees has long gone. Even checking out in the supermarket is largely done with a debit card or contactless. Because money is becoming more and more digital, it is harder to have good insight into your income and expenses. That is why it is becoming more and more important to properly manage your money flows. If you have good insight in how money flows, this gives you peace of mind. In other words, how does your Titanic sail? Don't run your Titanic into an iceberg. In an iceberg, the biggest danger is hidden underneath the water's surface. Look underneath your financial situation so you can sail around the undesirable financial setbacks. Whatever you do, make sure you have enough lifeboats for everyone.

By paying attention to your financial affairs, you show that you respect money. The word *respect* is used in many different ways and in many different places. In most cases, it is about the respect between people, but why do people have so little respect for money? Money is frequently spent recklessly, wasted in a meaningless manner. By throwing away and wasting money, you show that you don't respect money. You owe your money and your possessions the attention they deserve. Everything you nourish, grows, and that also goes for money. Respect and manage money in a good and wise manner, and you will watch it grow.

BANK Management

You have mapped your own start and end situation, and you know how much money is coming in and where it is going. This has had to do partially with the past. The bank management focuses on your future. What does your future image look like? In other words, how will you ensure the safe voyage of your Titanic? You will open a different account for each letter in bank. By opening different accounts, you can properly organize your money flows. Sticking to the bank management system requires discipline, but don't punish yourself if you fail at times. Be mild to yourself and accept your situation.

Every bank account has its own purpose. Some accounts will be used more frequently than others. The important thing is to have all four accounts and to actively use them. Using four active accounts is simplified by automatic bank transfers. Immediately after your salary, or any other income, is deposited into your bank account, automatically transfer part of it to the other bank accounts. How much you transfer to each account depends on your situation. You will map your situation in the next chapters. I will now discuss the four bank accounts you will open.

The B in bank management stands for buffer. You will subdivide your buffer into two numbers: one part is for big expenses, the second part is for your fixed expenses. The A stands for assets. How do you form your possessions, and what do you pay attention to when forming possessions and what kind of possessions suit you best? The N stands for normal expenses, regular expenses that are daily, weekly or monthly in nature. In conclusion, the K stands for kindness. Kindness also consists of two elements: being nice to yourself and to others.

Good bank Management

As you know, I used to own an online bookkeeping suite and administration office. Both the bookkeeping suite and the administration office focused on freelancers. This mean that, in addition to bookkeeping and company finances, I did tax returns. That's how I met Kristel. She applied the bank management system really well. She opened four private bank accounts and monthly transferred fixed amounts to the four accounts, as private income.

After a year of saving, she had a sufficient buffer for all regular expenses, and the amount to be transferred was reduced to the height of the reservations for big expenses. The amount she saved with regard to regular expenses was added to the account for possessions. That way, Kristel wanted to grow towards a situation in which she became less and less dependent on a job. Every month, Kristel donated a fixed amount to alternating charities and a fixed amount to fun things to do. Fun things can be going out to dinner, a fine glass of wine, a visit to a museum or a day at the beach. This makes life much more pleasant, especially if they are successes you can celebrate.

Life Without Bank Management

Going through life without bank management results in a lot more stress. Because of my experience at my administration office, I have been able to see a lot of personal finances of people. Because he is ashamed about his own situation, I will name the person in the following example Peter. Peter had no overview of or insight into his financial situation at all. His credit card was used to the max, plus he had store cards that allowed him to shop on credit. To make things worse, Peter had discovered mail-order companies. They deliver on account and allow you to pay in installments. Because of this, you won't notice the effect of your purchase on your wallet until much later. To complete the disaster, Peter loved a good meal and had expensive taste. It doesn't take much to guess that after a while, Peter was knee-deep in financial difficulties. He was unable to resolve it on his own, and he was forced to enable debt remediation. They mapped everything for him, and he was given a weekly allowance to survive. It felt like a total humiliation to him. He learned the hard way and he applied the money method. He is now learning to live with money and working toward bank management.

Insight into your money flow prevents you from having to calculate continuously. If you're not calculating to make sure everything is covered, you are worrying about money matters. Break this negative spiral with the help of bank management. Imagine how much time you will have left when you aren't calculating all the time, no longer robbing Peter to pay Paul. Worrying about money matters has no use at all. What positive things could you spend all this free time on? Thinking about how to increase your possessions becomes a luxury problem. Worrying about money leads to nothing. In yourself, in the money method, you were given a number of techniques to help you stop worrying. Use them to give yourself peace of mind.

Take Control

Bank management gives you control over your own financial movie. If you have control over your own matters, this leads to peace of mind. No more hidden icebergs underneath the sea level. In case you didn't miss the iceberg, you have a solid buffer that helps you deal with it. The ship doesn't sink, you can proceed to sail towards the nearest port and repair the ship. Take control over your money flow, regardless of how large your money flow is. A major blow for one can be a minor setback for someone else. For instance, if you have a brand-new car and you dent it, you probably consider that to be a significant ordeal. But if you drive an old car, it doesn't really matter; it is mildly unpleasant. As long as you have enough money to deal with a major setback, you will definitely want to have a dent in your brand-new car repaired.

Before I started my own company, I was the person responsible for finance at companies of 200-600 people. On a weekly and monthly bases, I was in touch with the entrepreneur about his finances. Just like with a freelancer, the private situation of this entrepreneur was discussed. My former boss had so much money that he never had to work again, nor did his children and any grandchildren. His net value was in the millions. One day, we were discussing the figures of his company. The company was doing well. Then, we discussed his private situation. He shared with me that he felt like he had no money left at all. The company was invested in various holdings and he had given a large portion to his children. He thought he had lost everything because he had given away so much and the money was in his companies. He didn't consider the money in his company as his money. His companies were worth millions. It cost me a lot of time to convince him of his amazing financial situation. I had to go straight against his feelings about money. This is how, even if you're extremely rich, you can feel very poor.

Put the bank to work, to manage your money. Allow them to do their work, to give you maximum insight into and overview of your money flow. In the next four chapters, I will extensively explain what belongs with what bank account. This allows you to properly distribute your income across four accounts of the bank management. After introduction of the system, you will have time left, which you can then spend on other things. A good implementation of bank management will help you get your financial affairs in order in an easy and practical manner.

Summary of BANK Management
- The emergence of money
- Open four different bank accounts
- Regain control of your money flows
- You manage your money, not the other way around

Forming a buffer is an important part of bank management. As soon as you have a buffer, you will experience the calmness it brings you. In the next chapter, you will calculate the height of your buffer and work towards it.

Chapter 10

B–BUFFER

A budget is telling your money where to go
instead of wondering where it went.
—**Dave Ramsey**

When writing this book, I encountered Karin. I told her about bank management. She connected multiple meanings to the word "buffer." The conversation made me write again and introduced me to the following most common meanings of the word buffer. The most common meaning of the word originates from the ICT industry. A buffer is a temporary storage on a computer. In bank management, your buffer also is a temporary storage, only here it concerns money. A second meaning of the word buffer is bumper. If you have sufficient money in your temporary storage, you can take a hit.

As soon as you have a solid buffer, this will have a great effect on your brain. Having a buffer will significantly reduce the time you currently spend on worrying about money and on calculating. If you spend this time on positive matters, your emotions will improve. Imagine what having a buffer would do for you. Visualize what it feels like to have a buffer, a bank account with sufficient money to account for planned expenses. Your buffer will give you peace of mind as soon as you have built a solid one. It will greatly improve your mood. Building and maintaining your buffer requires discipline. It is extremely easy to transfer money from your buffer account to your account for normal expenses or kindness. Don't be tempted, and make sure to replenish your buffer after you have taken a hit. There's a good reason why bank management begins with a buffer. A buffer gives you peace of mind.

I had an extensive conversation with Karin about the buffer. Initially, we spoke about the meaning of the word, but also about what size a buffer should be. Karin believed that an absolute amount should be attached to the size of a buffer. The size of your buffer depends on your situation. For instance, if you live in a big city such as New York, your buffer will be different than someone living in Thailand. Additionally, your standards for living will also impact your buffer amount. Everyone's buffer is different.

The Two Elements of a Buffer

Two elements are required to calculate the size of your buffer. The first part of your buffer will consist of a reservation for major expenses. Major expenses are those that you do several times a year or just once a year. The most common example of a major expense is a car. Almost nobody buys a new or second-hard car ever year. You buy a car with the intention of driving it for a couple of years. In the time between the purchase of two cars, you spend money on fuel, insurance and taxes. These costs are part of your normal expenses, which will be discussed in a another chapter. Throughout the years, the period in which you drive the car, you will have to make your buffer grow until it is big enough to buy a new car.

The second part of your buffer consists of a building sum of 6 to 9 months of your normal expenses. You don't want to get in trouble if you have to live without income for a certain amount of time.

Major Expenses

To concretize your image of major expenses, a number of examples have been included. In the previous paragraph, the purchase of a car was discussed. A car is a tangible thing. You can save for a distant journey, such as a trip around the world, or a visit to a friend or a family member who lives far away. The trip itself requires solid planning, as do your financial reservations for this trip. Doing a study involves costs. A good study often costs a lot of money and time. Tangible major expenses include expenses for a kitchen, bathroom or furniture. These expenses are in your long-term planning. Your medium-long-term planning contains matters such as a laptop, refrigerator, television and a home theater set. Everything that will be spent within 12 months falls under short-term planning and with that, your normal expenses, even though that vacation you plan once a year can be very expensive.

6-9 Months Savings

In another chapter, I will extensively discuss the height of your normal expenses. There is a good reason for choosing this period of 6-9 months of expenses for your buffer. Bad things happen to everyone, like losing your job unexpectedly, for instance. If you don't have a buffer, this immediately causes double the stress. When you lose your job, you also lose your income. People need about 1 to 2 months to recover from a major setback. After this first shock, a period of reflection begins. "What do I want the rest of my life to be like?" is a frequently asked question. This period generally lasts 2-4 months. Subsequently, you need another 1 to 2 months to shape your new life. Depending on your own pace and the gravity of the incident, 6 to 9 months will have passed before you know it. If, during this period, you don't have to worry about your income, you are free to do as you please. You can go in any direction, not inhibited by stress or coercion due to your financial situation.

Find Your Buffer

Whether you need a big or small buffer depends entirely on your own situation. Do you own a lot of expensive stuff that has to be replaced every couple of years, or do you live simply and minimalistic? Do you want to buy everything new or is second-hand good enough for you? You can make this decision per object. Walk through your house and see whether you need everything. This way, you can reduce your buffer for your major expenses. Start by making a list of stuff you have in and around your house that will survive longer than a year. With every item, write the replacement value and the year of replacement. I have included a sample buffer calculation for you here.

Housing	Expense	Life cycle in months	Months until replacement	Buffer size
Kitchen				
Bathroom				
Roof				
Painting the house				
Garden				
Garden home/shed				
Swimming pool				
Window frames				
Doors				
Pavement				
Central heating				
Total investments in your house				

Transportation	Expense	Life cycle in months	Months until replacement	Buffer size
Car				
Motorcycle				
Boat				
Bicycles				
Total investments in transportation				

Appliences	Expense	Life cycle in months	Months until replacement	Buffer size
Refrigerator				
Dishwasher				
Deep freezer				
Television				
Sound system				
Alarm system				
Laptops/computers/ printers				
Total investments appliences				

Other	Expense	Life cycle in months	Months until replacement	Buffer size
Education				
Training				
Traveling (not annual holiday)				
Total other investments				

Total buffer size large expenses	

Total buffer size normal expenses	

TOTAL BUFFER NEEDED	

Based on this overview, you can calculate how big your buffer for major expenses should be. Don't forget to include big trips and studies in your overview. At the end of the chapter, you'll find an example calculation of your buffer for major expenses. In a next chapter, normal expenses will be discussed. Your normal expenses depend on your income, where you live and whether six months are enough for you or that you'd rather go for nine.

Sit down on a chair and straighten your back; place both feet on the floor. Imagine your own buffer. Close your eyes and feel what it would be like to have a buffer. Keep this up for 5 minutes and experience the peace of mind a buffer gives you. Write down how this change makes you feel. What thoughts do you have after visualizing having a buffer? Be aware of your current situation and accept it without judgment. Don't look back, and begin building your future. It is ok if building a buffer is hard. Focus on the process from now to the final stage of your buffer. Having a buffer in itself is not the goal; the road towards it will give you more and more satisfaction. Make your planning and celebrate your successes in realizing your planning. Do not get mad at yourself or get frustrated if you don't always make it.

Summary of a Buffer
- What is a buffer?
- Determine the height of your buffer
- What are the two elements that together form the buffer?

Everyone could and should invest in assets. Up to a certain point, the following claim is true: "The bigger your assets, the less worries you have." There will be a moment when the asset glass will overflow. Think about all the good things you can do with the surplus money.

Chapter 11

A–ASSETS

*Someone is sitting in the shade today because
someone planted a tree a long time ago.*
—Warren Buffet

Assets covers everything that is your property. In assets, any debt is initially ignored. If you have the full right of use and ownership, it is your possession. You are free to do with it as you please. You can sell it to someone else without any problems. Your possessions can be diverse. This includes all tangible goods in and around your house. If you have a second home or a boat, these are part of your assets too. Your bank account may not be tangible, but you can make it tangible. The same goes for your equity portfolio. Whereas you used to have paper shares, nowadays this is all digital. In conclusion, there are various intangible things. For instance, you may have a patent or a concept or idea registered. Selling this isn't always easy, but they do represent a value you can count as your assets.

Opposite to your possessions is your debt. The most common and largest debt is the mortgage on your house. The value of your house is part of your possessions, and your mortgage is opposite to that. These two are inextricably connected. You are allowed to use your house; it is your property and you can sell it. With the proceeds of the sale, the mortgage must first be paid. Expensive purchases are frequently financed by the selling party. For instance, you can buy a car on down payment. You borrow money for your car. The same applies to mail-order companies. You can pay immediately or choose to distribute payments across multiple months or years. Don't forget to include your credit card debt. People pay by credit card, which isn't deducted immediately from your bank account. In the end, you still have to pay. In conclusion, there are also bank credits and loans. How much are you in overdraft, and how high is your bank loan?

Paying off Debt

Debt needs to be paid off as quickly as possible. Not all debt is easy to repay. In particular, the obligation that comes with your own house is a long-term obligation. I would not recommend selling your house and paying off your mortgage. You are probably enjoying your house in a way that can't be expressed in financial value. The crisis in the housing market has caused a lot of mortgages to be higher than the sales return of the house. This means that selling it would leave you with residual debt. This is not a desirable situation. All other debt can usually be paid penalty free. Make an overview of all your debt and the term of your loans. Now that you have this mapped, you can add all interest percentages.

You have generated an overview of all your debt, terms and associated interest percentages. It is shocking to find out how much interest you pay your credit card company. Mail-order companies and their rates can shock you as well. The interest rates they use are just below the credit card level. Calculate before you spend money, check how much interest you are about to pay. Don't look at the seemingly low monthly amount you are going to pay. Being in overdraft at the bank is very costly as well. Next are the long-term loans at the bank. The lowest interest rates apply to mortgages. The difference is that, in case of a mortgage, your house serves as collateral for the bank. As soon as you are unable to meet your payment obligations, your bank will confiscate your house. If you have a credit at institutions that use a lower interest rate, use that credit line to pay off institutions that have a higher interest rate. This way, you pay much less interest. The best thing still is to pay off debt as soon as possible.

Building Your Assets through Investments

As you are paying off your debt, you will also start building your possessions. Don't wait with this until all debt has been repaid. Give your possessions the attention they deserve. Everything you pay attention to, grows. It is wonderful to see how you can make your possessions and assets grow. In fact, your possessions can make you money. It doesn't matter what amount you use for your first investment, as long as you invest. Every invested amount will give you something in return, which will give you significant satisfaction. You didn't have to do anything for the extra amount, but it is in your account. If you are able to work on increasing your assets, there will be a point at which you can live off of the income from your assets. In this case, you have created the perfect situation for yourself. You are free to do whatever you want, without worrying about your finances. In fact, you don't have to do anything at all.

Investing can be done in many different ways. Begin with an investment in something that interests you. This is a world you understand, a world in which you can't be fooled. Further explore the market you're interested in. There always is more information available that you currently don't have. Consciously choosing certain investments, or refraining to do so, is an important success factor. A second success factor in investing is spreading your investments. Don't bet all your money on one horse. Should that one investment go bust, you won't have lost all your money. Draw up an investment strategy in advance. Without a strategy, you run the risk of investing in sectors you don't know much about. Determine your strategy and stick to it. One final bit of advice: don't let the market pace get to you. If something decreases in value rapidly, don't sell and take your loss right away. This is a guaranteed loss. Go for the long-term and not for short-term profit or loss.

Below, I have listed some possible investment opportunities to help you grow your assets. They're in order of risk, from low to high, the idea being that you can invest with the level of risk you feel comfortable with. The most important thing is that you invest in *something*.

Currency

Trading in currency can be done via your broker. I recommend against having currency in your home in cash, unless you have a big and secure vault. A lot of national currency moves with relatively small jumps. That is why investing in currency involves little risk. Local governments are behind their own currency and issue guarantees for their own currency. New crypto coins, however, involve a greater risk.

Bonds

A bond is a loan to a company. You pay a one-time amount to a company, and you receive an annual fixed interest percentage in return. Once a year, a fixed number of bonds is randomly selected. If your bond is selected, you get your money back. As long as your bonds are open, you receive interest. Over time, bonds can be converted into shares. A bond that can be converted into shares is called a convertible bond. You hand over your bond, usually pay something extra, and get shares in return.

You have converted your loan to the company in shares, and you have become co-owner. Bonds are also issued at a small scale. There's a beer brewery for instance that has issued bonds but does not pay interest. If you have a bond in the beer brewery, you are given a beer package on your birthday. This is a creative way to refrain from having to pay interest. They do randomly select a number of bonds every year, because the loan is repaid eventually.

Real Estate

Investing in real estate has experienced a lot of peaks and valleys in recent yours. The biggest low point was the international crisis that started in 2007-2008. Make no mistake, investing in real estate is not easy. You are owner of a house or apartment with the intention of renting it out. The perfect situation may be a holiday cottage at the sea, which you can rent out throughout the year and occupy yourself for a couple of weeks a year. If you like DIY work, this is a perfect solution; however, you don't want to spend your entire vacation doing chores and maintenance. If you outsource everything, it won't make you a lot of money. Another way of investing in real estate is trading in real estate. Knowledge of the local housing market is a requirement. It is possible to buy a house cheap, fix it and then sell it again at a higher rate.

Crowdfunding

Crowdfunding is considered a relatively new and low-threshold investment method. However, crowdfunding isn't as new as it may seem. The best example is the Statue of Liberty in New York. France gave the Statue of Liberty to New York, but the pedestal that had to carry it, had to be paid by the city itself. The associated cost was $ 250,000, but initially, the city was unable to raise more than $150,000. Subsequently, the owner of a newspaper company launched a crowdfunding to raise the remaining part of the $100,000. This amount consisted of tons of small amounts for a larger goal, such as the pedestal. This is how crowdfunding works nowadays as well. You lend money to a company or you receive a share of the company in return. Companies you invest in are usually small- to medium-sized companies. Listed companies have other ways to get money from the market. You, as an investor, can use crowdfunding to easily invest in or lend to companies. Thoroughly investigate the company you want to invest in, and spread your investments.

Shares

Investing in shares is a relatively easy way to invest. You open an account with a broker and you're ready to start trading. Trading via a broker is required in the stock market. Say you work in ICT, for instance, and you want to invest in shares; you need to find an ICT company. Look into a number of similar ICT companies. Look at the figures from the published financial statements and the future expectation of the company. Choose the company you think is a good investment. I can't give you an entire investment course in this book. If you want to invest in shares, I recommend taking a course or explore the matter thoroughly yourself.

Raw Materials

When it comes to trading in raw materials, people generally only think about gold. However, there are plenty of other raw materials you can trade in. Metals, such as silver, platinum, palladium and copper are in high demand. Trade in oil is well-known, but cacao, coffee and sugar are also popular raw materials in trade. If one of these goods has your attention and interest, this might be an option for you.

Cryptocurrencies

Bitcoin is the most famous crypto coin at this point. This currency is not supported by governments, nor are they covered by a gold reserve. Trade in this currency if entirely based on mutual trust and confidence in the market. These courses fluctuate significant, depending on international new coverage. The question is: how much confidence do you have in these new crypto coins? Do you dare invest in them or not?

Explore Your Market

The most important thing about investing is exploring the thing you want to invest in. Read books on investment opportunities of interest. Do plenty of research online. This prevents the purchase of an empty shell, as a result of being conned by unreliable people. Be cautious of people who want to take the investment off your hands, promising sky-high returns. The pyramid scheme of Madoff is a well-known example. By robbing Peter to pay Paul, he managed to embezzle $65,000,000,000. Be careful with what you invest in.

If you don't care much for investing, just leave the money in the bank. You'll get a fixed interest and often, the government guarantees a certain amount, should your bank go bankrupt. A bank is the best guarantee for your money, but it also has the lowest return.

Summary Assets

- Calculate your possessions
- What is the height of your debt?
- How will you pay off debt?
- The various interest rates
- Types of investment
- Choose the investment that suits you
- Explore the backgrounds of your investments

Regular life must continue. The normal expenses are required for that. You control the height of the expenses that are part of your lifestyle.

Chapter 12

N–NORMAL EXPENSES

Being frugal does not mean being cheap!
It means being economical and avoiding waste.
—**Catharine Pulsifer**

I n the Hollywood principle, you have described your own movie. What did the past 12 months look like and what does the movie of your future look like? In this movie, various expenses pass review for recurring items. Whether you like it or not, you will always have normal expenses. How high these normal expenses are is different for everyone. Everyone has a different lifestyle and associated spending pattern. It's good to explore what you consider to be normal expenses. It is useful to explore the use and necessity of frequently recurring expenses. Take the past, analyze the past, correct in the present and work on your golden future. Be honest toward yourself, look in the mirror and don't brush up the past. Your ego will try to apologize for expenses that were useless. There's no need to defend yourself, to apologize or to explain why you made certain purchases in the past. Accept your own impulsive purchases from the past. Focus on your future.

You have mapped the past. It is now time to shape your future movie. You decide what this movie will look like on the big screen. How does your ship sail to America? How will you avoid every iceberg? How do you reach the safe port in America? It doesn't matter if you are the financially poor Jack or the financially wealthy Rose. You need to live your most beautiful and best movie, regardless of what others think of it, including your own ego. It is your financial situation; you know how much is coming in and you know what you need.

A Millionaire's Expenses

Conscious millionaires have a standard of living below their income. Normal millionaires will rarely have expensive cars in their driveway. The extremely rich, however, will. In addition, millionaires spend a lot of money on traveling and gaining experiences. The fixed expenses of a villa are higher than a small apartment on the third floor. The same applies to the cleaning expenses of a pool. Millionaires eat out more than others. Their clothing style varies from expensive brand clothing to clothing that everyone wears. Millionaires spend more on clean technology. Charity is an important expense of millionaires. Just look at how much money Bill and Melinda Gates donate to charity. Warren Buffet has given away the majority of his capital. Warren Buffet isn't your standard millionaire. He drives his own car, he never travels with a private jet even though he owns an airline company, and he has a relatively low salary for a CEO. He advises youth to stay away from credit cards and to invest in themselves.

The Average Joe's Expenses

Your average Joe is working hard to make ends meet every month. He owns a house or lives in an expensive rental with monthly payments.

This forms a large portion of his expenses, in addition to the daily groceries and fixed expenses associated with the house. His car forms another large expense. He can save up for one or two vacations a year. He likes eating out a couple of times a year. He has enough money for his hobbies. In general, Joe does not have enough of a buffer to allow him to take hits. Joe can deal with a setback, but if he suffers more than one, he has a problem.

Common Expense Types

Whether you live like a millionaire or like an average Joe, you will spend money in several common areas, like housing and food. Whether your home and meals are extravagant or modest, you may need to prioritize these expenses. It starts with understanding how you currently spend your money and how you want to prioritize your spending in the future.

Housing

The biggest expense in many households is housing. This can be monthly rent or interest and mortgage payments. Monthly interest belongs to normal expenses. Mortgage payments reduce your debt and therefore they are part of assets, not normal expenses. Expenses for gas, water, electricity and insurances are normal expenses. These are regular expenses that recur monthly. Small maintenance to your house is categorized as normal expenses. Determine how much money you spend on housing each month. Copy this in the overview at the end of this chapter.

Groceries

Daily groceries can vary per person or household. Whereas one household spends a lot of money on food because they have an expensive taste and frequently eat steak or attach great value to organic food, the other household goes for discounts. In practice, organic food is more expensive than regular supermarket food. Everyone is free to choose brand products or white label products. Always pay attention to the quality of products. Eat well, healthy and varied.

Insurances

Home insurance and contents insurance are part of your housing expense. There are more insurances, such as your healthcare insurance. Worrying about your financial situation is one thing, but worrying about your health is worse. If you are healthy, you have a thousand wishes. If you are not well, you only have one wish. You can insure all you want, but always consider the usefulness and necessity of your insurance, in relation to the cost associated with an incident. I used to have legal insurance. After years of paying premiums, I had a question. I was snubbed, because they said they didn't see any reason to have my question answered. I immediately cancelled my insurance and started putting away the premium for the insurance myself. About 10 years later, I had another legal question, but by then, I had money put away to cover it.

Clothing

You frequently need new clothes. Whereas some people buy new clothes as soon as old clothes are worn-out, others want a new wardrobe as soon as the new fashion is released. Everyone has their own spending pattern; don't judge the spending pattern of others. It is unpleasant when others immediately form a snap judgement about you. Second-hand clothing stores are for people who are unable or unwilling to spend a lot of money on clothing.

Travel expenses

Travel expenses go beyond your car; otherwise, they would have been called car expenses. In a lot of households, the car expenses are the largest expense when it comes to travel. Driving a car is an expensive hobby. Varying from fuel to insurance. Depending on the age of the car, you will have frequent maintenance expenses for your car. Everyone uses public transportation now and then. Include an amount for public transportation. In conclusion, we have the bicycle. Your bicycle requires frequent maintenance. Your car, public transportation and your bicycle are common means of transportation. And we can come up with a lot more. What other means of transportation do you use? Calculate the expenses for each of them.

Financial Obligations

You pay interest on your debt. How much interest you pay per month depends on the kind of debt it is. Only the interest component falls under your financial obligations. Debt payments are also financial obligations but are eliminated against possessions in this overview. First pay off, then keep saving. Optimize your loans and pay as little interest as possible.

Personal Care

Caring for yourself is extremely important. Take good care of yourself and you will be able to take care of others. Cost for personal care consists of frequent purchase of products such as toothpaste, shampoo, soap etc. The visit to your hairdresser or your beautician are also part of personal care. A lot of people benefit from a pedicure, acupuncture and other healing methods that are not covered by health insurance. Expenses for your gym or sports associations lead to god health and are part of personal care.

Education

You need to keep developing yourself nowadays. Reserve time and money to be able to continue your studies. This can be both a study for your company or profession, but personal development is just as important. People frequently respond to this by saying: "But all these studies are so expensive." If you think that knowledge is expensive, try finding out how much ignorance costs. You can learn without money. You can always go to a library to borrow books, schedule time to read them. Another option is to sign up as volunteer for a course you want to attend. You provide services, while learning.

Other Expenses

We have listed eight categories, but we can come up with so much more expenses that someone might have. The described eight categories are expenses that exist in almost every household. It is your creativity in your own expense pattern to place all other expenses you may have under this heading. Make sure that you categorize all expenses, and if you are left with expenses that don't fit any category, create a new one or put it under other expenses.

Overview

Collect all expenses from these categories. Copy them into the following overview, so that you have a good idea about your expenses. You now know what your normal expenses are. Take a critical look at your normal expenses. Are there any expenses that can be eliminated? If so, eliminate them immediately!

Compare all expenses you mapped to your income. You know now how large the portion of your buffer must be to be able to live 6 to 9 months without other income. Include this amount in your buffer. If there is nothing left, if you spend more than you make, it is time to increase your income or reduce your expenses. Take action immediately.

You have your income, minus your normal expenses. An amount remains to be distributed among your buffer, your possessions and kindness. All items from bank management must have an amount or percentage assigned to them. At the same time, build your buffer and your assets. Don't forget yourself and others, be kind to yourself and to others.

Summary of Normal expenses
- It is about your life standard, now and in the future
- Determining your expense pattern: millionaire, Joe Average or minimum
- Thoroughly go through your expenses and assess your expenses based on usefulness and necessity
- Make an overview of your normal expenses
- Calmly go through the list and see what you can eliminate

Kindness is the next chapter. How can you be nice and to whom are you nice. In any case, be nice to yourself, you'll see that the people around you will be a lot nicer to you.

Chapter 13

K–KINDNESS

Financial peace isn't the acquisition of stuff. It's learning to live on less than you make, so you can give money back and have money to invest. You can't win until you do this.

—Dave Ramsey

A re you a giver? If you are able to give, you will lead a more satisfactory life because you are more connected to your environment. You may feel a process of giving and receiving being established. This encourages you to give more. You may feel reluctance to give. If you give something away, you'll have less of it yourself. The fear of losing out may be a reason to be reluctant in sharing and giving. You are afraid that sharing will be at your expense.

If you share in full and without reservations, you encourage generosity among others. See how you relate to the giving issue and discover, when you don't want to give anything, how you confirm yourself in this presupposition. Sharing is multiplying.

You can give in various ways. You can give attention, make knowledge available, share your material wealth, and more. The question is, how does giving make you feel? If you share information and display your own experience, you encourage others to share what they know. The reciprocity of sharing knowledge or time will be present all around you. Above all, you will be a happier person if you can help others with your knowledge or your time.

Be Kind to Yourself

Take a good look around you. By that, I don't mean your literal surroundings, but mainly people around you and those you interact with. Place yourself in your circle, as a separate personality, between people who are already present in your circle. How kind are you, as a person, to these other people. Are you kinder and friendlier to others than to yourself? People have the tendency to punish themselves harder or to demean themselves. If someone else near you makes the same mistake, are you more forgiving to them? Or to yourself?

If something goes wrong, think to yourself how you would judge if someone else had made the same mistake. Your forgiveness towards others generally is much greater than to yourself. As soon as something goes wrong again, treat yourself the same way you would treat your best friend, being kind to yourself, you'll become a more positive and optimistic person. Don't torture yourself on your own mental rack. Your own ego, your own brain, is the one punishing you so hard. As soon as you notice that your ego is punishing you, you thank your ego for its assessment and go on with your life. Leave the assessment of your ego for what it is, correct what went wrong and proceed without any negative feelings. Accept what happened and don't judge.

Be Mild to Yourself

Being kinder and milder to yourself are an extension of one another. Where being kinder to yourself is in the past, what went wrong in the past, being milder to yourself lies in the future. Your ego comes up with expectations for your future. These generally are unrealistic expectations. Unrealistic expectations for yourself and others in the future, cause stress. Imagine that you can't meet your own expectations. The voice inside your head will say, "I need to make it, or else..."

Be milder to yourself if you don't meet your expectations. You don't have to adjust your expectations. Setting goals and visualizing them is important. Torturing yourself for not having met your goals is useless. Be mild to yourself and have faith in yourself. Look at the new you, the one who is mild to himself. Imagine not meeting a certain goal and not punishing yourself for it; it will make you a better and more satisfied person. You radiate this onto the people around you and they will reply with the same mildness.

Take Care of Yourself

Taking good physical and mental care of yourself is healthy. Body and mind are inseparable. If you are physically healthy, this benefits your mental health. I recently spoke to an acquaintance of mine who had gained 55 pounds in a year. I had not seen him for about a year, and I wondered why he had gained so much weight. He used to have a reasonably athletic body and he used to be a cheerful person. Now, a year and 55 pounds later, he no longer had any energy and he was complaining about everything and anything. Complaining and making excuses will lead to nothing. Fortunately, he found his way back to the gym. Six months later, I ran into him again, 33 pounds lighter and much happier.

In addition to your physical health, take care of your mental health as well. Seek education and personal development, which is the best food for your mind. If you keep learning and developing, your brain will remain active. An active brain can help you achieve a lot. Your brain decides who you are and what you do, you can positively deploy your ego. Say the following out loud: "I am the master of my ego, not the slave of my ego." If this becomes reality for you, the people around you will treat you better.

Be Kind to Others

What you give, you'll receive at some point. It starts very simple. Try and give someone a compliment. If you feel reluctant to give others a compliment, start giving yourself a compliment. The next step is to give a compliment to someone close to you. If you like yourself and you give others compliments, the people around you will like you better as well. The people around you will start paying you compliments as well. These compliments will make you happier and nicer to others.

In addition to giving compliments, having a smile on your face is also good for yourself and others. People get happier if they hang out with people who are happy and cheerful. That's how easy it is to be both kind to yourself and to others. If you want to go even further, volunteering is a great option. You are directly helping your fellow man. There are few tasks that are more rewarding than helping others. Never done this? Start small to get used to it, and gradually take bigger steps.

Give to Others

Moneyfulness actually gives money to organizations that fight poverty. By means of these donations to projects you'll find at www. Moneyfulness.me, Moneyfulness contributes to a better world. Look around you and see what you could do with money. Choose projects and organizations that pursue goals close to your heart. Help these organizations complete their project. How would it be to see the realization of the project happen? It doesn't have to be major and compelling things. Help a neighborhood association from your own neighborhood and see what happens.

Give More than Just Money

As previously described, doing volunteer work is a great way to do more than just give money. Volunteer work in the broadest sense of the word, from getting groceries for your neighbors because they are unable to do so, to the chairmanship of your tennis association. All people who spend their free time to help others. In addition, there are countless of organizations who ask volunteers for immediate help, varying from youth associations that are looking for leaders to the elderly who would like to go out in a wheelchair but are no longer able to do so themselves. Another way to help is not possible for everyone, but it does have great effect. If you have the talent to speak in an inspiring manner, you can inspire entire populations. A well-known example of this is Bono, the lead singer of U2. He has used his fame, his stage experience and his network to give a very inspiring speech about poverty elimination. This speech is available on the YouTube channel of TEDX. Check out his speech and be inspired.

Examples of Kindness

Role models are important to shape and change yourself. To concretely shape kindness, so that you will get the entire picture, I have gathered various examples. Famous people serve well as role models, because it's so easy to identify with them. Every role model contributes to poverty reduction, each in their own way.

All examples have two things in common. For starters, they are all people with a great drive and passion, and they all pursue their big dream. By passionately pursuing their dreams, they have gotten this far, and they have gathered their wealth. The second similarity is they use their name and financial resources to improve the world. They try to eliminate poverty with just as much passion as they used to get famous. Get inspiration from these examples, so you can see them as role models.

Bill and Melinda Gates

Bill is an entrepreneur, founder of Microsoft and expert in the field of ICT. He was born in 1955 and discovered his passion for computers and programming at a very young age. Together with his friend Paul Allen, he wrote computer programs for the Lakeside School where he was enrolled. Bill didn't complete his education at the time, because he was more interested in computers. He started Microsoft and led the developments of DOS for IBM PCs in the early eighties. Microsoft launched the first version for the general public under the name Microsoft Windows in 1985.

Melinda was born in 1964 and developed an interest in computers at a very early age. She got her bachelor's degree in computer science and joined Microsoft as product manager in 1987. She stayed with the company until 1996.

The Bill & Melinda Gates foundation is the largest foundation in the world that aims to eliminate poverty and illness. The text below is one of the key elements the foundation believes in:

> *The path out of poverty begins when the next generation can access quality healthcare and a great education.*
>
> *In developing countries, we focus on improving people's health and wellbeing, helping individuals lift themselves out of hunger and extreme poverty. In the United States, we seek to ensure that all people—especially those with the fewest resources—can access the opportunities they need to succeed in school and life.*

Bono

Bono was born in 1960 and joined the band U2 when he was still in high school. It wasn't until the 6th album, *The Joshua Tree*, that U2 became an international sensation. There are plenty of nominations and awards to underline the quality of U2.

Everyone who follows Bono even a bit is aware of his involvement in global issues and knows how much he commits to that. *The National Journal* has named Bono "The most politically effective celebrity of all time." One of the things Bono commits to is poverty elimination. He does so in various ways, for instance, through the "Keep a child alive" project, which addresses the hunger problem in Africa.

Michael Dell

Michael Dell is the entrepreneur who partly shaped the PC revolution in the eighties. Michael Dell was born in 1965. When he was twelve years old, he took a job as a dishwasher at a Chinese restaurant, which allowed him to buy a computer when he was fifteen. He wanted to buy a computer to take it apart and see how it worked. When he was in college, he came up with the idea of selling PCs directly to consumers. Computers had to be affordable for everyone. He started building his own computers and selling them to people in his immediate vicinity. Just like Bill Gates, Michael Dell dropped out of college, because he wanted to start his company.

The focus of the Michael and Susan Dell foundation is on increasing access to education throughout the world. In particular, they care for everyone who has a disadvantage compared to the majority. Breaking this vicious cycle of poverty combined with better healthcare and education of children is the top priority of the foundation.

Earvin "Magic" Johnson

Magic Johnson was born in 1959. After two years of college, he was scouted by the Los Angeles Lakers, for whom he played thirteen years and won the NBA championship five times. Personally, he was given the title "Most Valuable Player of the NBA," and he was elected into the Naismith Memorial Basketball Hall of Fame.

Magic Johnson Enterprises is an organization that focuses on investing in retail projects in low-income neighborhoods. Examples of projects are cinemas, restaurants and gyms. The goal is to improve the quality of life in poor neighborhoods. Through project development, Magic Johnson contributes to happier lives of people in disadvantaged neighborhoods, and in doing so, he fights poverty.

Scarlett Johansson

Actress Scarlett Johansson was born in 1984 and is known for movies such as *Hitchcock* and *The Avengers*. She comes from a poor family and started her acting career with a role in *The Horse Whisperer* when she was just thirteen years old.

Scarlett is active within Oxfam, the power of people against poverty. As an Oxfam ambassador, she has traveled through India and Sri Lanka. Blessing in a Backpack mobilizes organizations, communities, and individuals to put together food packages for children who are starving during the weekend. This is part of the activities of the USA Harvest program. The third program for which Scarlett commits is Soles4Souls. Shoes and clothing are collected and distributed across the world.

Ben Affleck

Author, producer and writer Ben Affleck was born on August 15, 1972, and he can't remember that he ever wanted to be anything else than an actor. His breakthrough was together with Matt Damon in the movie *Good Will Hunting*. Afterwards, he played various major roles. For his production *Argo*, he won a Golden Globe award and a BAFTA for Best Director, Academy Award, Golden Globe and BAFTA for best movie.

Ben Affleck supports a large number of charities in various ways. One of the charities he actively supports is Feeding America. One in eight people in America is hungry and needs the foodbank to survive. Ben Affleck is very committed to those who are hungry. Check videos of Ben Affleck for Feeding America on YouTube.

Angelina Jolie

Angelina Jolie was born in 1975 in Los Angeles. She has won three Golden Globes and an Oscar. Her international breakthrough was in 1997. *Forbes* declared her to be the best paid Hollywood actress in 2009, 2011 and 2013.

When she was filming *Tomb Raider* in Cambodia in 2000, for the first time, she became conscious about the worldwide humanitarian crisis. She learned more about the humanitarian crisis and contacted the United Nations/UNHCR. She's visited a lot of refugee camps. Angelina Jolie is very engaged in getting the politicians to act in favor of the refugees. In 2012, she was appointed Special Envoy of the United Nations High Commissioner for refugees.

Summary of Kindness

- Sharing is multiplying
- Share something other than money
- Be as kind to yourself as you are to your best friend
- Take good care of yourself
- Be nice to others
- Give to others and to charity
- Giving makes the giver happy
- Famous role models care about giving and contributing
- Choose your role model

If you are a mindfulness trainer or coach, the following chapter is interesting for you. If you are a coach in the field of personal finance and would like to know more about the world of mindfulness, continue reading and discover the other field. This applies to everyone who wants to have the link between Moneyfulness and mindfulness explained further.

CONCLUSION

Step 1: Congratulate Yourself and Celebrate!

The first real step was buying this book. Congratulate yourself for getting to the end of *Moneyfulness*. I hope you have carried out all assignments. If you have carried out all assignments from the Money Method, you may still worry about money at times, but your stress about money has disappeared. With the help of the Hollywood principle, you have mapped your past and a part of your future. bank management helps you secure your financial future. Celebrate the path to financial peace of mind and independence. Treat yourself to something nice or fun; don't let the moment go by unnoticed!

Step 2: Make a Plan and Carry It Out

As a result of the exercises from the Money Method, your attitude towards money has changed. Your money stress has disappeared, and you now know how to manage your finances. Make a detailed plan of how you are planning to implement bank management in your daily life. Make a plan, carry it out and stick to it. Everything depends on the actions you take. The more closely you follow the instructions from Moneyfulness, the better it will work. Get up and take action!

Appendix A
MONEYFULNESS FOR MINDFULNESS TRAINERS

When writing this book, various mindfulness trainers were approached to see whether they saw something in the idea of Moneyfulness. First, the response was mainly negative: money is not the problem. In itself, this defensive attitude is easy to understand because the stress factor of "money" does not exist in mindfulness. Without elaborating on the term "Moneyfulness," stress concerning money will not be reflected in mindfulness training.

Marriët Reijnders is a psychologist and mindfulness trainer. Together, we have developed the live training mindfulness.

Moneyfulness as a Supplement
Money is consistently in the top three of things people worry and stress about. The other two are relationships and work. Work can be subdivided into stress associated with the work itself, such as an unpleasant boss,

and losing your job. Losing your job is inextricably connected to losing your income.

Worry and stress are the results of regret about things of the past or about uncertainty in the future. By staying in the here and now, you reduce stress. If you are currently sitting on a chair, and if you don't think about things you bought or future expenses, you will automatically experience peace of mind. The thoughts and doomsday scenarios do not affect how you feel at this single moment. As soon as you go back in time or anticipate financial issues, stress presents itself.

Moneyfulness is a supplement to existing mindfulness trainings. There is overlap in the approach of both trainings. Supplemented with practical tools about how to deal properly with money. A small study conducted in-house shows that current mindfulness trainers spend little to no attention to money. Because money is in the top three of stress and worry, it should be a part of mindfulness. That is why Moneyfulness was created, as a supplement to various existing mindfulness trainings.

Mindfulness in Moneyfulness

Chapter 1 specifies the seven aiding factors of mindfulness. Based on these seven principles, I will show you how mindfulness and Moneyfulness are connected and supplement each other. Similarities between all seven aiding factors and Moneyfulness are reflected in the Money Method. Based on the Money Method, the aiding factors are assigned.

Mindset

In the mindset of the Money Method, you'll find the most connections with mindfulness. For starters, there's "acceptance." Be willing to see your own reality. How have you currently organized your finances? Don't be angry or frustrated if your current situation is not your ideal or desired situation. The number of people that are on the right track right away is zero to be precise. The second factor is "letting go." Be aware of your thoughts, ideas, wishes, opinions, hope, experiences from the past, etc. You have been formed by your past, which has brought you to the current point in your finances. This is neither good nor bad, it simply is what it is. If you experience resistance against money or claims and statements about money you're struggling with, acknowledge this resistance and struggle and try to stop it. The third factor is "Beginners mind". Begin your financial future with an empty sheet. Write your own financial future. Send your Titanic where you want it to go, to your port, navigating between the icebergs you are bound to encounter.

Opportunities

Life is full of opportunities. You simply need to wait until the idea presents itself to you. When the time is right, you must be prepared to seize that opportunity. Frustrations about not having found your cash cow yet are not useful. It will come when you're ready. The aiding factor "patience" fits opportunities of the Money Method.

Not judging

A factor literally adopted from mindfulness is "not judging." Don't judge and condemn others. Don't be blinded by apparent riches of your fellow-man. Don't try to compare yourself to your neighbor, who has a more expensive car. Don't discard your neighbor as a show-off because he has a more expensive car. Look at your own car and be content with it. Observe what you have. The trick is to not be affected by the outside world, because everything happens in your mind. Don't judge and condemn others based on what you see on the outside.

Empowerment

"Non-striving" is the aiding factor of mindfulness that goes with empowerment. There is no other goal in life than to be yourself. Do things you like, that give you energy, and best case scenario: put you in a flow. In the kindness examples, you'll find famous world citizens. Every single one of them started by pursuing their passion and dream. Then, fame and money followed. Be the best version of yourself.

Yourself

Have faith in yourself and in your feelings. Be confident that things will present themselves when the time is right. Trust yourself and have faith in yourself. "Trust" as an aiding factor, goes with yourself. No reaction without action. Take action to work on yourself and keep learning. Change your inhibiting convictions and realize what you want to realize. Analyze yourself and your behavior with the help of the eight money archetypes. If you improve your strong money characteristics and avoid your pitfalls, you can increase your confidence.

All seven aiding factors can be used in the Money Method. It is easy to make a connection to mindfulness with it. The interpretation of the aiding factors from mindfulness are used differently in Moneyfulness because money virtually doesn't exist in Moneyfulness.

Money as an Entry Point

There hardly is any attention to money in mindfulness. With that, the door for certain types of participants remains closed. Money issues, as a starting point for a training, opens these doors. Various studies shows that money does cause stress, anxieties and depressions and can literally make you sick. In addition, your IQ drops over 10 points when you are stressed for a prolonged period. By identifying money as a problem that is mainly in your mind, you can better help people. In the beginning, you won't find a lot of people who dare or are willing to specify money as a cause of stress. Money is not a common entry point for mindfulness trainers. Because money is in the top three of stress factors, it is worth considering it. To each their own, but being of service to each other can't hurt anyone.

Current Group of Participants

After a brief investigation among mindfulness trainers, four main groups were identified of people who sign up for mindfulness training. Depressions are an important reason to follow a training. You want to get rid of your depression and lead a happy life, and regain control over your life. The second reason are anxieties. Anxieties relate to possible things, whether or not realistic, that might happen in the future. A third and important group addresses stress and burn-out. If you are exposed to stress on the job for a prolonged period of time, you can suffer from burn-out. As soon as you have fallen into a burn-out situation, your brain is unable to think clearly. The last big group suffers from chronic physical conditions. How to deal with their issues?

As you can see, the four main groups cover two of the three elements from the top three of worrying and stress. Financial matters are not addressed in the current training program of mindfulness trainers.

Potential Group of Participants

Once someone has attended a Moneyfulness training, proceeding into mindfulness or providing support in personal finances is easier. The group that does have money worries but has never linked it to Moneyfulness. Very down to earth people with ordinary people problems, a money deficit, the wrong mindset with regard to money or inhibiting convictions about money. By making a combination between the seven basic elements of mindfulness in the Money Method and the practical application of the Hollywood principle and bank management, you lower the threshold to mindfulness. The Money Method in itself is a practical application of aiding factors from mindfulness. Outsiders consider mindfulness to be woolly, but it doesn't have to bee. This is the label slapped onto mindfulness by people on the outside. It is much easier to pass snap judgment and acting accordingly than to first neutralize the emotion and refrain from acting.

Evidence-based Moneyfulness

Mindfulness attaches great value to underlying theories being evidence-based. It doesn't matter whether you give trainings based on mindfulness-based stress reduction (MBSR) or based on mindfulness-based cognitive therapy (MBCT). Moneyfulness is a new concept that has not yet been subjected to independent scientific research. There has however been research into the relationships between money and stress/worry/not judging/giving. Money is the number one cause of stress and worrying in the United States. There are plenty of Mindfulness articles that demonstrate the positive connection between not judging and mindfulness. By concentrating on and accepting your own financial situation, you will have less stress. Don't join the rat race; follow your own path. In conclusion, there is a positive correlation between giving and your wellbeing.

Below you'll find a number of articles and studies that demonstrate the connections between money and stress/worry/not judging and giving.

Substantiation Moneyfulness—Stress

In America, money issues are number one in the list of stress causes. APA (American Psychological Association) performed a study in 2014 among 3068 adults of 18 years and over. According to this study, financial issues can significantly affect health and wellbeing. 72% of the group [that was part of the study experienced financial stress in the past month. Financial issues keep some Americans from going to the doctor, which constitutes an immediate health risk. Almost a third (31%) specifies money as an important cause of relationship conflicts.

http://www.apa.org/news/press/releases/2015/02/money-stress.aspx

The US National Library of Medicine and the National Institutes of Health has conducted studies into the correlation between money and stress. The conclusion is that money is the main cause of stress.

Various studies have consistently shown that income and status derived from a job are the two main factors of wellbeing (Deaton 2012). The influence of your financial situation on your health and wellbeing has often been studied from various disciplines, including social psychology (e.g. Anderson Kraus, Galinsky & Keltner 2012) sociology (e.g. Whelan 1992, Whelan & Maitre 2007) economy (e.g. Boyce, Wood, Banks, Clark & Brown 2013) Health psychology (e.g. Adler, Epel, Castellazzo & Ickovics 2000) and gerontology (Chou, Chi & Chow 2004, Litwin & Sapir 2009)

> https://www.ncbi.nlm.nih.gov/pubmed/27400815

Substantiation Moneyfulness—Worrying

A new neuroscience study reveals what worrying about money does to your brain. Neuroscientist Sam Barnett lifts a bit of the veil on making financial decisions. These tests were carried out with the help of an EEG scan. The study shows that a small push in the right direction or a demarcation of your choices, results in much less stress. Barnett divides income and expenses in three clearly defined groups. bank management has four clearly defined groups for dividing your income. Without help or registrations, you'll experience 20% more stress when making financial decisions. That is why bank management is such as useful and convenient tool.

> https://www.forbes.com/sites/elizabethharris/2017/11/28/new-neuroscience-study-reveals-what-worry-about-money-does-to-your-brain/#fc0e19385e9d

Substantiation Moneyfulness—Judging

A study from 2010 published in *Mindfulness Magazine* suggests there is a relationship between judging and stress, anxieties and feelings of depression. Judging less equals a lower level of stress, anxieties and depressions. In the study, the awareness and non-judging thoughts are the main predictors of wellbeing. Don't judge about anyone's financial situation based merely on what you see. Only the tip of the iceberg is visible. You don't know how many loans someone has taken out to keep up appearances. Don't join the rat race to keep up with others in purchasing tuff or distant travels. Look at your own situation, accept it and adjust your expenses. Be aware of your finances and accept others as they are, without judging.

https://www.mentalhelp.net/articles/the-impact-of-judgmental-thinking-on-your-anxiety-and-depression/

Substantiation Moneyfulness—Giving

According to a study carried out by Dunn, Aknin and Norton, giving will make you feel happier. The higher the percentage of income donated to charity, the happier you'll be. In the field experiment in which they were asked to donate $ 5 or $ 20, independent of their own income (they were given money and allowed to donate) it turned out that donating 5 or 20 dollars did not make a significant difference.

https://www.huffingtonpost.com/brady-josephson/want-to-be-happier-give-m_b_6175358.html

The feel-good effects of giving begin in the brain. It's called "giver's glow," says Stephen G. Post, director of the Center for Medical Humanities, Compassionate Care and Bioethics at New York's Stony Brook University. The response, he says, is triggered by brain chemistry in the mesolimbic pathway, which recognizes rewarding stimuli. Philanthropy "doles out several different happiness chemicals," Post says, "including dopamine, endorphins that give people a sense of euphoria and oxytocin, which is associated with tranquility, serenity or inner peace."

This pleasure and reward system evolved some 1 to 2 billion years ago, and at its most basic level, is tied to the joy we receive from eating, sex and social interactions. Viewing the brain with MRI technology during moments of generosity or selfless behavior has led scientists to uncover that even the thought of giving can engage this ancient response.

One study published in 2013, in the *American Journal of Public Health*, found that giving time and assistance to others reduced the mortality risk tied to stress, a known risk factor for many chronic diseases. According to the study, which looked at 846 adults in the Detroit area, stress did not predict mortality for participants who had helped others within the previous year. But the link between stress and mortality was apparent in people who didn't lend a helping hand, even after adjusting for age, health and other variables.

https://health.usnews.com/health-news/health-wellness/
articles/2015/05/01/what-generosity-does-to-your-brain-and-life-
expectancy

Training Moneyfulness for Mindfulness Trainers and Personal Finance Coaches

Are you convinced of the stress factor "money" in the life of a large portion of your students? Attend a course "Teaching Moneyfulness." Your point of departure depends on your expertise. If you are a mindfulness coach, you will mainly learn about the financial field. If you are a personal finance coach, you will learn mainly about mindfulness. The perfect situation is to give tie course with two people, in which one has a mindfulness background and the other has strong personal finance skills. What's important is that you can replace one another. Learn about each other's world and benefit from that. Take the course and gain the license to teach Moneyfulness trainings in your own area. If there already is a Moneyfulness trainer in your area, contact him / her to see whether you can work together.

Summary Moneyfulness for mindfulness trainers
- Moneyfulness is a supplement to mindfulness
- The seven aiding factors from mindfulness translated into Moneyfulness
- Money as a problem, as a cause of stress
- Substantiation Moneyfulness stress
- Substantiation Moneyfulness worrying
- Substantiation Moneyfulness not judging
- Substantiation Moneyfulness giving

Many mindfulness trainers/coaches are also entrepreneur. The next chapter is about the application of Moneyfulness in entrepreneurship. As you may know, I developed an online bookkeeping suite and established administration offices in a franchise formula. My first book was written for entrepreneurs who want nothing to do with their bookkeeping. Based on the NUMBER method, you'll be able to organize your administration and gain financial insight.

Appendix B
MONEYFULNESS FOR ENTREPRENEURS

Freelancers

Every freelancer needs to keep track of his finances. Nobody else can keep track of your finances in such an organized manner as you. You can of course hire an accountant or administration office. In all cases, you are responsible for your administration. In any case, you need to be the one billing, nobody else can do that for you. In the NUMBER method, I will explain a way to keep track of your numbers to gain financial insight. In addition to the book about Moneyfulness, I have written a book about finances for freelancers called *Ik heb niets met cijfers* (I'm not a figure person). This book was written for people who are not interested in figures but who have to work with them anyway. The majority of these readers will consist of freelancers who came from a work situation in which they only needed their specialism.

Freelancing requires more than that, such as having a solid administration. When you have a specialism without figures, this isn't easy. Support is desired. With this book, I hope to take away all questions and insecurities with regard to your administration, so that everyone can get started, whether you are a figure person or not.

You don't have to become a specialist in the financial field, but I do recommend having optimal insight into your figured. Nobody can tell you anything; you are at the helm of your company.

Entrepreneur

If you are owner of a medium-sized company with employees, you probably have someone who does the administration for you. The person who takes care of the administration for you is the financial conscience of the company. You, as an entrepreneur, must be able to fully rely on your employee. You hold this employee fully accountable for the financial state of affairs. Say you get a tax audit. It turns out that things didn't go entirely as they should. Your employee didn't do it on purpose, but you have to pay the fine. Or even worse, your company is doing so badly, you risk going bankrupt. By the time a company might go bankrupt, decisions are made, in particular in the financial field, that may not all be sound.

Both in the case of a tax audit and in case of an imminent bankruptcy, you, as an entrepreneur will always remain responsible for your administration. In fact, the management of large multinationals are ultimately responsible for the finances of the company.

A well-known example of this is Enron. In the nineties, the core activity moved from supplying gas to trade, selling and buying term contracts. A lot of money can be made in that, but a lot of money can be lost as well. Enron always managed to dodge the bullet during audits, because there were hundreds of subsidiaries, all with shady constructions. By convincing the outside world of the success of the company, millions of dollars were paid in bonusses to the management. However, the company would soon turn out to be 20 billion dollars in the red. In December 2001 Enron went bankrupt, and suddenly, 21,000 people lost their jobs. After the bankruptcy, a criminal investigation was launched. All upper management of Enron were held jointly and severally liable for fraud within the company. Jeffrey Skilling and Andrew Fastow were respectively sentenced to 24 and 10 years in jail. Director Kenneth Lay died of a heart attack, briefly before his ruling. Another manager, Clifford Baxter, committed suicide. The accountant who had worked on all constructions, Arthur Andersen, had issued an approving statement for the financial statements, even though it was crystal clear there was something wrong with the books. It turned out that Arthur Andersen had destroyed many documents. As a result of the Enron scandal, the company Arthur Andersen ceased to exist.

Duplicate

Regardless of the size of your company or the company you manage, you are the one ultimately responsible. You will always be held accountable for hits responsibility. When everything is going great, there won't be any problem. As soon as things go wrong, people will knock at your door. It generally isn't easy to hold an accountant or administration office accountable for mistakes they make. They draw up a financial statement based on the data you provide. If you don't provide everything, they cannot be held liable for errors. In advance, you sign a LOR (Letter of Representation) in which you state that you have provided everything.

Apart from everything that can go wrong, back to your administration. It isn't relevant where or by whom our administration is done, as long as you have insight into it. As entrepreneur, you need to have financial insight in two places: at home and in your company. A tip I would like to give you, is that you can project the overviews of your private situation almost literally on the finances of your company. Freelancers in particular know exactly how much money is made and spent at home. As soon as it concerns their company, they have suddenly lost all overview and bookkeeping is considered to be something difficult. Compare both financial overviews and find the similarities. As a freelancer or entrepreneur, keeping track of your finances in duplicate cannot be avoided.

Good Bookkeeping

You need to do your bookkeeping, and if you do, you might as well do it right. Bookkeeping is considered to be a cost item, but better would be to see it as information provision. In fact, bookkeeping is nothing more than processing all financial mutations. This can be done both manually and digitally, although a fully digital administration is preferred. Throughout the year, your bookkeeping mainly consists of four types of bookings. You buy services or goods (purchase invoices), you sell goods and/or services (sales invoices) and you receive and pay money (bank or cash bookings). Finally, there are other bookings, such as salary and depreciations.

If you receive a purchase invoice digitally, make sure to immediately store it in the folder "To be booked." If you receive the purchase invoice on paper, make sure to digitize it by means of a photo or scan and save your invoice in said folder. Log into your bookkeeping software every two weeks and book the purchase invoices that need to be booked. After booking, drag your digital invoices to a folder named "Booked." Do this every two weeks to make it part of your routine and so that you gain insight into amounts to be paid.

Every entrepreneur likes making sales invoices. This is a financial reward for your work. Log into your bookkeeping software every week and make your sales involves. The foundation for these sales invoices is different for every entrepreneur, registration thereof is at your own discretion. As long as you send invoices every week, your money flow remains constant.

Book your bank statement every other week. By updating your purchases biweekly, your sales weekly and your bank statements biweekly, you gain good insights into any amounts to be paid or received. Every other week, you'll see the development of your outstanding items. You can track your bank balance daily or weekly through the app of your bank.

Finally, you'll have other bookings left that need to be booked once a month or once a year. Depreciations will be once a year, just as transferring your annual result to your equity. Your payroll journal entry, an overview of all salary costs of your staff, must be booked monthly. All other bookings take place in the memorandum.

NUMBER Method

The NUMBER method is a method that helps you gain insight in figures. This method consists of six steps. The first step is to properly reconfigure your computer. Use a fixed folder structure and you will have no problems finding everything you need. Subsequently make an inventory of what elements are part of an administration. Your administration as a whole is a broad concept. It covers everything you document.

Always keep in mind that this is your administration. It is and will always be your sole responsibility, regardless of who does the work. If your administration is up to date, you have financial insight and overview. There are various ways to obtain this insight. The economy has a lot of angles. A lot of these angles have been described, as well as how you can make your economy grow. How you, as an individual, can affect the economy.

The realization is the final part of the NUMBER method. This is an implementation in six steps:

Note your accounts:	As an entrepreneur, you are responsible for your own administration. In the example of Enron, you have seen that you will always remain ultimately responsible for your administration.
Unite your data:	What does your administration cover? Make an inventory of everything associated with your company. This will give you a good idea about the state of your company. When making an inventory, it's not just about administrative documents, but about all activities of your company. What are you currently doing? What is your expertise and how do you sell it? What documents do you record?
Map your device:	Organize your computer in a structured manner. Use a computer to organize your own data as good as possible. It doesn't matter whether you're using a laptop or a desktop, as long as it is comfortable for you to work with. A tablet is possible as well, if it easy to make a folder structure on it.
Balance your finances:	Know your figures and learn how to read and interpret them and provide key figures. Insight into your own finances and result is important. The main reason to have good financial insight is you. In addition, there are bodies who required you to have a correct administration. I am mainly talking about the tax department and the Chamber of Commerce. Good financial overview means you have insight in your figures and are not blindsided by large

expenses such as investments, your VAT return or your income tax declaration. If you don't reserve money for these major expenses, you will face a serious issue at a certain point. You have a money deficit, but you have to pay nonetheless.

Economy: The economy in general and your economy in particular. The entirety of trade in goods and services across the world is generally referred to as the economy. Usually, transactions are completed with money, in all possible currencies. One party sells something and is given money as an interim tool. That money can then be used to buy something else, for which you have to hand over the money. Money is the perfect interim tool. You can use money to make more money, by lending it or investing it in commodities such as gold or in companies. This form of capital growth is part of the economy. There is a macro economy, micro economy, political economy and your personal economy.

Realization: How can you organize your administration? Bill weekly, book your purchase invoices and your bank / cash mutation biweekly. Pay bills that are due every other week. Put money aside for VAT and your income tax every month. Book your payroll cost and depreciations every month. Close your financial year within 4 weeks after the end of your financial year.

The purpose of the NUMBER method is get the hang of an administration without too much effort. By that I mean administration in the broadest sense of the word. You will be guided and informed about what action is required when and how to perform this action. The six steps have been designed in a logical manner. At the end of the process, you will have applied a clear structure in your work method, due to which your administration is a piece of cake.

The structure and work method are a combination of simply doing things with the right mindset. The NUMBER method will have to be applied a number of months to actually be part of your system. It helps you do your administration in a structured and simple manner in as little time as possible. Cutting your bookkeeping time in halve is an important goal, as is doubling your financial insight and overview. Everyone can do bookkeeping; I am convinced of that. Whether you actually *want* to do your bookkeeping is entirely different question. However, that you *have* to do something with your figures, is a fact. By making your bookkeeping as easy and accessible as possible, the threshold to start working with your figures is reduced as much as possible.

Financial Statement

In the financial statement, a difference can be made between a private company and a sole proprietorship or partnership. A sole proprietorship and a partnership have no obligations regarding the financial statement. There are no requirements with regard to a financial statement they have to provide. In your income tax declaration, you must provide the tax department both with your income statement and your balance. According to law, you are free to do whatever you want with your figures, but the tax department forces you to use a certain format. The financial statement is a piece of history and is pleasant to have as a reference. A financial statement forces you to look at the financial consequences of your company at least once a year.

Depending on the size of your company or the type of activities, having an accountant approve your annual figures may be a requirement. Go to this meeting well-prepared and don't get overwhelmed by technical terms. Be aware of what happens within your company in terms of finances.

Balance Sheet

When checking your balance, your comparison to the Hollywood principle will begin. A company has a start of the fiscal year and an end of the fiscal year. Whereas, in the Hollywood principle, you can choose where your movie begins and ends, for your company this has been predefined, A fiscal year usually is identical to a calendar year. Because the majority of the companies has configured their bookkeeping like this, this is the basis.

Your possessions are on the assets side of your balance. What does your company own? In the display of your balance, it no longer matters whether it concerns a private company or a partnership. Two moments of your assets are important: January 1st (start balance) and December 31st (end balance). What happened in the meantime is not interesting for your balance.

If you would list a balance horizontally, your possessions would be on the left. The asset side of your balance covers all possessions booked positively. These are possessions or claims on third parties. In summary: the property of your company. If all possessions from your company are sold, a bank balance will remain. Some items are easier to sell than others, selling everything is a theoretical approach.

In addition to possessions, a company also has debt. This is listed on the credit side of the balance, and can have various name: debt, liabilities, and credit amounts. For reasons of convenience, I will use the term liabilities in this chapter. Your liabilities must be in balance with your assets.

If you would list a balance horizontally, your liabilities would be on the right. Often, your assets and liabilities are shown vertically in a financial statement. In the classic system, your assets and liabilities are listed next to each other. A balance must always be in balance; the value of your assets must be equal to the value of your liabilities.

Equity is listed on the debt side. A lot of entrepreneurs consider this strange. It is my company, and my equity, isn't it? And yet, it still is on the balance as debt. To thoroughly understand this principle, it is easier to see you and yourself as two different elements. From the perspective of your company, the equity of your company is debt to you, as owner of your company. In other words, you, as a private individual you have a claim against your company.

Income Statement

For the income statement, I will return to the Hollywood principle. Your income statement tells your story, your movie between the opening shot and the final shot. It is a sum of everything that happened in your company during the year. Everything costs money or generates money.

Cashflow

The cashflow overview is an overview in which your actual money flow is displayed. The cashflow overview shows what you spent your actual Euros on last year, as an entrepreneur. The cashflow overview relates to the past. A cashflow projection shows the expectations of your future financial resources. By understanding the past, you can better predict your future.

A cashflow overview is not related to the operating result. The flow of your financial resources is connected to the operating result, but there are various affecting factors at play that have nothing to do with the operating result. A general rule is that, if you make profit, your cash and bank balance will rise. This is no guarantee. A cashflow overview is a collaboration between your income statement and your balance.

'Cash is King' is a frequently heard statement. If cash is king, this underlines the importance of this overview. Regardless of how the company is doing, if you are out of cash, you will still go bankrupt. You can make a profit and still go bankrupt because of a lack of cashflow. On the other hand, there are plenty of examples of IPOs or crowd funding instances in which a lot of money is collected, but not a single dime is made. A well-known example is the company Uber. In 2016, Uber achieved a turnover of 20 million dollars, but suffered a loss of 2.8 billion dollars (2.800.000.000 to indicate the size of the amount). Regardless of the massive loss, the value is estimated at 69 billion. Uber is not listed but has a number of investors who supplement the deficits.

Financing

There are various reasons to request financing. One reason may be the purchase of a building, expensive machines, installations or a company car. These are tangible fixed assets. You may be growing right now. If you need to keep products in stock, your stock may be growing faster than your bank balance. Financing a stock is very common. The third large funding group concerns working capital financing to cover your current payments.

Establish in advance how much money you need: borrowing too little will get you into trouble. At a certain point, you will suffer a deficit. Borrowing too much isn't smart either, you'll pay more interest on your loan compared to the interest you receive on your current account. Excess liquidity is doing nothing on a bank account. Over-financing will not be approved by a financier.

The period during which you need the money is often connected to the purpose of your financing. If you are purchasing a building, the period will be twenty or thirty years. If you have stock financing or working capital financing, your financing period will be much shorter. The period during which you need the money depends on your repayment capacity. How fast can you repay a loan you have taken out?

Using Moneyfulness in Your Company

After the substantive part about the finances of your company, the question arises how to use Moneyfulness in your company. In your balance and income statement, I made a bridge to the Hollywood principle. By properly comparing your business and personal figures, you will find a large number of similarities. Approach your business figures like you approach your personal figures.

Because of the comparison between business and private, you can use the Money Method for your company. Model the Money Method in such a way that it applies to your company. In your mindset about your income, how you deal with customers is addressed. What is your attitude and mindset towards your customers. On the other hand, you spend money on suppliers. How do you deal with them? Is it easy for you to pay them, or is it always hard for you to transfer money to your suppliers?

To clarify the use of Moneyfulness, I will give you a description of an entrepreneur who uses the Money Method. Without repeating the entire Money Method. Only bridges to the Money Method and supplements can be added as an entrepreneur. This is not exhaustive, there are endless supplements to entrepreneurship, based on Moneyfulness.

Mindset

Peter is an entrepreneur and a freelancer. He carries out ICT projects at large-sized companies. Peter is a wonderful professional, he loves his job. Every week, bills have to be sent. Currently, Peter is being confronted with the hourly wage to be billed. Peter starts getting nervous and starts sweating. Can he bill this amount? It is a very high amount. Am I worth this? Did I work hard enough for it? When Peter negotiated this hourly amount with his principal, it seemed like a low amount, it was only an hour. But now that everything is added up in an invoice, the amount has become extremely high. The mindset of Peter with regard of his own value is not as it should be.

Maarten, however, loves billing; after all, he worked hard for it. The best thing for him is to actually see the amount being deposited on his bank account. Every day, he checks whether his principals pay him and he jumps for joy when he receives money. He is grateful towards his principals, they are the ones who pay him to do what he loves to do.

After billing, you need to collect. Every entrepreneur faces that one customer who doesn't pay on time. You have to contact your principal to ask for your money. Money you are entitled to. Many entrepreneurs freak out when they have to chase down their money. How high is your threshold for asking your principal about your money?

In addition to receiving money, you will also be paying money. In the description of the eight money types, you have found out what kind of money type you are. Suppliers want to receive money for the products or services you have bought. Is it easy for you to pay your bills, or are you having a hard time pressing "submit" when you are paying bills? Do you forget to pay the bill, leading to problems?

In the Hollywood principle, you have started working on your future movie. These were the personal goals you want to realize. How about your business goals: have you clearly visualized them? How great would your movie be if you have more money coming in and less money going out? Make such a planning, both in the form of the operating result and cashflow forecast. Be aware of your own mindset with regard to planning the financial future of your company. If you are having a hard time making a financial forecast, tell someone with a financial background the story of your company. They can perfectly translate your story into a forecast. It is up to you to go through the forecast and to assess whether everything you have told them is included in your forecast.

Opportunities

As soon as your company is temporarily not doing so well, insecurity strikes. You start wondering about the "why" question. Why are customers not coming back, why are there no new customers, why are existing customers buying less, etc.

To address the worrying, you can do the same exercises for your company as you did for your personal situation. Worrying is negative energy and only costs you time. Convert the worrying into positive energy and start looking for opportunities. If you start using worry time to get the why questions answered, you'll reach surprising insights. Investigate. You can also use the time you gained to look for opportunities. Talk to people inside and outside of your circle. Make sure you have a clear story and go for it.

Not Judging

Look at your competitors, but don't judge your competitors. Don't compare your company to that of someone else. As soon as you do better than your competitor, the law of inhibiting lead takes effect. If you frequently compare your company to competitors, and you are in the lead, than this is an invisible handbrake. If you are behind on your competitors, don't get frustrated. Stay with your own company. Spend time on improving your company.

On the outside, you can't see how a company is doing internally. Everything can be rented, from the biggest and most impressive commercial buildings to the most expensive cars. Some companies want to own everything, other companies want to have everything leased or financed. Don't worry about the appearances of someone else (unless this is your core business).

Empowerment

As an entrepreneur, regardless of the size of your company you can most easily implement empowerment. In the Money Method, you have discovered where your strength and passion lie. What activities make you get in the flow? Proceed with these activities and expand them further. The empowerment exercises show what consumes the most energy. What makes you frustrated and what work do you keep postponing. There are plenty of freelancers who label things you consider to be energy consumers, as fun. Without having to hire staff immediately, you can hire these fellow freelancers to work for you. They do the work in half the time you do it, an often better as well. Spend the time you gained on your passion, your strength, your dream. By outsourcing work, you become both a happier and better person, while making the person you outsource your work to happier. You are not able and not required to do everything yourself.

In not judging, it is useful to refrain from comparing your own company to those of your competitors. In empowerment, you look for a successful company, which may not even be in your own sector, and study why they are so successful. Read biographies of successful entrepreneurs and be inspired by these stories. Gain strength from these stories to continue what you're doing.

Yourself

This chapter is about your company in which you, the entrepreneur, are at the helm. If you feel good and are able to handle your money well, this will be reflected in your company. The NLP techniques from the Money Method can also be used in your company. When doing business, you encounter unpleasant situations. Future scenarios are described that make you shiver and you face decisions that don't just affect you, but all your staff. You know what money type you are and where your opportunities and pitfalls are. Literally apply this to your company and your company will do much better.

Summary of Moneyfulness for entrepreneurs

- Entrepreneur with or without employees
- Money is important in two places
- A good administration is priceless
- The NUMBER method
- The comparison between your financial statement and the Hollywood principle
- Cash flow and funding
- The Money Method translated into your company

Appendix C
FREQUENTLY ASKED QUESTIONS

Moneyfulness is a new concept. The goal is to eliminate poverty. This is an ambitious goal in which I can use all the help I can get, including yours. By buying this book, you donate 10% of the purchase price to the Moneyfulness foundation. In addition to this book, there is an online course as well as live training sessions. 10% of the proceeds of all these activities are donated to the Moneyfulness foundations. Making direct donations is possible as well. The distribution of the funds is handled by means of assigned coins you can gather via an app and the site. Moneyfulness is about money, which is why we have made the elimination of poverty our main goal.

What is Moneyfulness?
Money is the main cause of stress in the United States. And yet, within the existing concept of mindfulness there hardly is any focus on money. Since the combination of mindfulness and money did not yet exist, this concept was created. Moneyfulness can be divided into the Money

Method, in which all seven aiding factors from mindfulness have been translated into money and the practical way to handle money in bank management. The practical part is greatly underexposed in the existing concept of mindfulness. Since, in addition to resetting your brain correctly, the practical implementation is imperative for eliminating money-related stress, this book was written.

I am great with money, so why would I read this book?
Do you know all there is to know about money and do you feel that you are great with money? If your fully convinced of yourself and of this claim, this book is not for you. In reality, the group that never worries about money, is a very small minority. Within the 5% of the richest people on Earth, there are plenty who have financial stress. Worries about retaining the money, about allowing capital to grow and about preventing arguments about the inheritance. The bigger the inheritance, the bigger the risk of family quarrels. Are you worried about money? If so, this book can help you make those worries go away or at least reduce them greatly. Dealing with money is an interesting hobby, one that you should definitely invest time in. Stressing about money is a waste of life. Valuable time you waste worrying, can be used positively to deal with money in a constructive manner.

I have no money, let alone money to spare.
Do you recognize this situation? If so, this book was written for you! With the help of Moneyfulness, you can create a better life for yourself, one without financial worries, without spending valuable time on worrying about money. It is not about the heights of the amounts, it is about your attitude towards money. Managing your money and dealing with it wisely. Every penny counts, even if you have just one cent a week to spare. Get rid of your inhibiting convictions about money or accept

them and learn how to deal with money properly. You may even start liking money.

At the end of my money, there's a lot of month left
Robbing Peter to pay Paul is a very common problem. The credit card is a proven method to postpone payments. Getting a loan is extremely easy nowadays. However, everything you borrow must be paid back. Depending on the interest rate, you'll have to pay back much more than you borrowed. Pleasure today, the pain is for later. Millions of people live like this and have money stress. Towards the end of the month, the money runs out and the worries start. How great would it be if you could stop worrying and start spending all that time on fun things, because you have your finances in order. Read the Money Method, do the exercises and apply the bank management to your finances, and at the end of the month, you'll have money left.

Do I have to become a millionaire?
By all means, you do not have to become a millionaire. Everything depends on your wishes and your spending pattern. If you live alone in a small apartment, you don't need a lot. I am not talking about your desires for the future, but about your current spending pattern. When you live in a big house and have three children that go to college, things are a little different. Your spending pattern changes with every phase in life. Moneyfulness has a twofold objective. The first objective is to fix your attitude towards money, to say goodbye to inhibiting convictions and to obtain self-insight about your behavior. The second objective is to map your finances and to plan and secure your financial future. Having a lot of money is pleasant, a 1 million bank balance is extremely pleasant, however, as soon as it causes stress in any way, it's not right.

Mindfulness is a little vague to me. Is Moneyfulness for me?
Moneyfulness has a practical approach. There are exercises concerning your convictions about money and you'll obtain self-insight about your behavioral pattern. Very recognizable and applicable. Organizing and planning your financial affairs can only be done using a practical method. Bank management is the way to organize your financial affairs. The seven aiding factors of mindfulness are used to shape the Money Method. There is nothing vague about money.

Can I apply my charity for funding?
In principle, any charity that fights poverty in the world qualifies for a listing on www.Moneyfulness.me. The project plan must be well-substantiated with figured. How much money do you need and how much are you asking the Moneyfulness foundations. If the funding has a deadline, this must be specified. When a contribution is assigned to your project, you are expected to provide information about the realization of the project once it is completed. What has Moneyfulness contributed to and how was poverty in the world reduced as a result of this contribution. As soon as the project is posted on the website, it is up to you to motivate everyone to save coins and to assign them to your project.

My Story and Why You Will Benefit from This Book.
After a false start with my education and work experience, I quickly made up for lost time, and then some. At the age of 21, I got the label "underprivileged youngster" slapped onto me, because I had no professional training or any relevant work experience. I was never without a job; I accepted various temporary jobs in factories and fulfilled my conscription at the medical troops. Subsequently, I was given the opportunity to study again. From that moment on, everything went smoothly. I got my diplomas and built a career for myself. Things

were going so well that, at the age of 30, I was the person ultimately responsible for the finances of a transport company with more than 500 employees. I fulfilled this role at various companies for a period of fourteen yours. Some bigger, some smaller. I fulfilled my part in society and automatically got sucked up in the rat race. At times I had more money than I could spend, and at times I was short on money. The spending pattern adjusted to the income.

Despite my generous salary, money stress always remained a constant at some level. I had to keep my job, otherwise I would have financial problems. If you don't pay the mortgage, your house is put up for auction. During the crisis, house prices experienced a 25% drop in the Netherlands, and in the Netherlands, you face personal residual debt when the bank forces you to sell your house. If you sell your house with a loss on your own initiative, the residual debt will haunt you as well. The pressure to keep your job and to keep your income at a steady level, was massive.

Still, I started feeling the urge to start my own company. Together with a partner, I started developing an online bookkeeping suite. He provided the programming knowledge, I provided the financial and business knowledge. After two years of development, the software was ready for release. We both quit our jobs and started our adventure energetically. In addition to the bookkeeping suite, I immediately founded an administration office for other financial services. After 3 years, the administration office was converted into a franchise formula of administration offices. After two years, my partner left the company, and a larger ICT company took over the management and development. For the bookkeeping suite, a crowdfunding campaign was completed successfully. I published my first book. For the outside world, things appeared to be going smoothly.

One day, I woke up and I had a strange realization. My company was not doing so well, and the debt had grown too big. But somehow, it caused me little stress. I started wondering how that was possible, no money and no stress. In the top three things people worry about all the time, and that cause people a lot of stress, money has a solid position, in addition to relationship and work. Why did that not apply to me this time? During all the years I had worked as an employee, I made significantly more money, I usually had a buffer, as well as financial stress. My company had a debt of $200,000 to third parties, and I had invested $125,000 of my own money and about $200,000 in work hours. I considered the investment into my company to be my biggest asset. Virtually all investments were made into the software suite. Banks finance software to a very limited extent. It sounds strange, but something holds no value to a bank if it isn't tangible. The money I had worked so hard for, had been invested in the company, and on top of that, the bank had given me a private loan of 40,000 Euro. If you have come up with something and are passionate about it, you hardly every quit while you're ahead.

In summary, I was in big trouble. What to do with my company? And how to get rid of the private loan of 40,000 with the bank? Somehow, the entire financial situation caused me little stress. I explored how it was possible that my head/gut was so calm through all of this. In three years ahead of this situation. I attended a number of courses in personal development, in which various elements of mindfulness were addressed. Then it suddenly hit me: all personal development courses enabled me to keep my brain calm and to keep my nerves in check, without too much effort or stress. This is something I wish for everyone. Even if you have little money or are short of money, experiencing little to no stress about it, is a step in the right direction.

I've had periods in my life with money and money stress. Never did I expect to have a period in my life without money and without money stress. Being short of money is not pleasant, it needs to be dealt with, having financial stress is not necessary. Worrying costs too much time, which is better spent on solving the money shortage. Are you someone who makes a good living but who still is short on money? Someone who has a lot of month left at the end of your money? If so, this book was written for you. Are you out of money or is there never any money left? If so, I recommend that you keep reading, because there is no reason for either situation. If you have money but are afraid to lose it or if you have other financial worries, you need to focus on the Money Method.

No Money, No Stress

Money is the biggest cause of stress in America. Living without ever worrying about money is a utopia. Dealing with money, properly managing money is a good thing, as long as the occasional concerns don't turn into worrying and stress. If you don't have many and it keeps causing you stress, you need to define a timeslot during which you work on your finances. This can be no more than once a week. Go through all your financial matters once a week, pay your bills, check your bank balance, transfer money to your savings account, work on your insurances, your pension plan, etc. Don't try to get everything sorted during the first evening, you are looking for peace, not for pressure and stress. Don't spend more than two hours per week on your finances. Processing payments is a recurring ritual, just like spending fifteen minutes thinking or Googling to see how you can increase your income. Of all administrative tasks that are left, you add just one every week. The 166 hours in the week that are left should not be spent on worrying about your money. Worrying about money is strictly forbidden during those hours. The only activity you can spend extra time on is increasing your income and even then, only if you like it and it gives you energy.

Not having any money does not equal financial stress. On the contrary. What's important is how you deal with your lack of money. It is about your attitude about money. How to drastically reduce the time you spend on worrying about money.

The way to stop financial joyriding is
to arrest the driver, not the automobile.
—Woodrow Wilson

Explanation Moneyfulness

Mindfulness is a generally known concept. Basically, mindfulness helps you reach a state of inner peace, deal with stress and fears, reduce worrying and try to not judge others. The top three that people worry about and that causes them stress consists of relationships, work and money. Within mindfulness, there is great focus on the first two, relationships and work. If you take a closer look at work, you can divide it into two elements. The actual stress a job causes as a result of the amount of work, an unpleasant employer or colleague on the one hand. On the other hand is the stress that is caused when you feel that you might lose your job. This second stress is directly related to stress about money. When you lose your job, you lose your income. If you look at it like that, money is responsible for half of all stress and worries.

Moneyfulness consists of two elements. In the first element, I will walk you through the Money Method. In this method, you will get to know yourself, your attitude towards money, your inhibiting convictions about money and how you deal with money. How can you reduce stress and worries about financial affairs? How can you let others be who they are and not judge yourself too harshly? Don't torment yourself with all kinds of useless negative thoughts, give yourself some space. Start working on yourself, and put a stop to stress and financial worries. You can't eliminate it entirely, but you can keep it in check.

The second part of Moneyfulness is the practical part. You map your own finances. After you have obtained insight into your past, you will use the bank management system to get your finances organized. This will give you peace in the financial area and it allows you to properly plan your financial future. This has nothing to do with the absolute amount you think you need, any amount will do.

Poverty Reduction

Moneyfulness is about money and your mindset towards money. You can feel poor and have a lot of money or you can have a lot of money and spend even more. In this case, you have a poor mindset. Another way of poverty consists of financial poverty. People who have taken a wrong turn and are in trouble. People who don't have a dime, who have to rely on the food bank or even worse, have to engage in dumpster diving. People who don't have a roof over their head and who spend their entire life living out of a plastic bag. These are two extremes, there are a lot of nuances in between. Millions of people have a lot of month left at the end of their money. Think about how they long for help in their poverty. Poverty is a perception. In truly poor countries, they have no food or clean tap water, this is a whole different kind of poverty.

Moneyfulness is about individuals who, one way or the other, want to obtain a different attitude about money. You want to adjust the perception of your own poverty. In addition to your own perception, you want to improve your financial situation. By buying this book or by attending the course, you contribute to poverty reduction. 10% of all proceeds of Moneyfulness go to poverty reduction. This could be a local project in your area, or a drinking water facility with clean drinking water in Senegal. Everyone has the opportunity to submit a project that fights against poverty. In addition to literally donating money to charity or projects that fight poverty, part of the money is spent on education. By teaching people to properly managing their finances, you contribute to poverty reduction. Education can be considered as preventive poverty reduction.

Worrying about Money Benefits Nobody

Everyone worries about money sometimes in the broadest sense of the word. There is nothing wrong with worrying about your own finances or your financial future once in a while. It becomes a problem if it turns into a weekly, or even worse, daily habit. It means that the "contemplation" has turned into "worrying and stress." Frequently worrying about financial affairs and your financial future contributes nothing to your happiness in life. To the contrary, it adds nothing to your life. Worrying about money only costs you time and energy. Worrying is done with your brain, which is a problem, because your brain is the part of the problem that consumes the most energy. Energy that is better spent on other things. As soon as worrying becomes a serious problem, it becomes stress. Short-term exposure to stress isn't so bad, as long as you give yourself a breather afterwards. In this case, your innocent contemplation leads to worrying to stress. This means that you have been under financial tension for a prolonged period of time. You have built your stress throughout the weeks, months, or sometimes even years. If you recognize this, the time has come to do something about this, before you go too far. Long-term stress-periods can lead to physical and psychological complaints such as anxieties and depressions. Be well-aware of the stage you are in now. The more you have advanced in stages, the harder it is to turn the tide.

An underexposed item of money-related stress is the IQ. Now, you might wonder what financial stress has to do with your IQ. The average thinking capacity of people is defined to be 100. Money-related stress makes your IQ drop by more than 10 points.[5] This means that financial stress causes you to make less thoughtful decisions, or even stupid decisions. Let's say that you have an IQ of 90, which is more than

---

5   https://money.usnews.com/money/blogs/my-money/2013/10/23/study-financial-stress-dramatically-lowers-your-iq

enough to lead a good life. Financial stress makes your IQ drop below 80, which can be considered educationally subnormal (partly dependent on other factors). This is another reason why worrying about money benefits no-one.

For Everyone Who Worries about Money

Everyone has a period in their life with too much focus on financial worries. For some of these people, there is light at the end of the tunnel at some point, and the worrying reverts to casual contemplation. For a very large group of people, worrying about money is a weekly or monthly activity.

My administration office gives me insight into all financial data of my customers, both business and private for the tax return. My customer Marc has his own company and steadily pays himself his regular compensation half-way every month. This compensation is almost equal to his profit. His partner, Eva, is employed and gets her salary at the end of every month. Marc makes a nice living and Eva has a great job. To put it disrespectfully, they are two very average people when it comes to income. Still, they worry about money, or better said, they worry about their lack of money at least twice a month. This happens just before Marc pays himself his compensation and the week before the salary of Eva comes in. At the end of the money they have a piece of month left. They are unable to make ends meet. They don't handle the money they make properly, and they have not built a buffer that would take away their worries. I was unable to get insight into the exact spending pattern, but it was clear that it exceeded their income. They may have inhibiting convictions, or they are individually constantly falling for the same pitfalls or are unable to protect each other for the pitfalls. The story of Marc and Eva is not exception, I have seen many of these stories pass review in my administration office.

Mindfulness and Moneyfulness Go Hand in Hand

The seven aiding factors of mindfulness have been translated into Moneyfulness. By making direct connections between both methods, they go hand in hand. Back to the top three of stress causes: relationships, work and money. Within mindfulness, there is great focus on matters such as anxieties, depressions, and burn-out. The stress caused by money is hardly addressed in mindfulness. This really surprised me during my research of the backgrounds of mindfulness.

The worrying and stress area of money is not touched by mindfulness. Financial worries are in the top three of all studies on stress. It could be that a top ten was studied, that contains two money-related topics, due to the highest just falls short of the top three. But add-up all money-related topics and it is solidly in the top three.

Since mindfulness and Moneyfulness are directly linked; they supplement each other. Moneyfulness enriches mindfulness. Because money doesn't exist in mindfulness, Moneyfulness was established and developed in addition. The two go hand in hand.

The Seven Aiding Factors of Mindfulness

For those who are less familiar with mindfulness, these are the seven aiding factors of mindfulness.[6]

1. Not judging: Don't judge others. Try to observe without judgment. It helps you "see" what goes on inside your head. Be aware of your own prejudice. The trick is to refrain from acting on your prejudice. What happens in your head, stays in your head.
2. Non-striving: There is no other goal than to be yourself, in any form.

---

6   http://www.mindfulness-meditation-now.com/support-files/seven-attitudes.pdf

3. Acceptance: The willingness to see things as they are. By accepting every moment completely as it is, you will be able to experience life as more complete.

4. Letting go: You have thoughts, ideas, wishes, opinions, hope, experiences, etc. These can be pleasant, or unpleasant. Stop resisting and stop struggling to achieve it and let things be as they are.

5. Beginner's mind: Let go of all your past and start fresh. Be open to all new things and allow yourself to be surprised.

6. Patience: Things happen when the time is right. Don't be frustrated because something doesn't work the way you want it to. Be patient. In time, all pieces will fall into place.

7. Trust: Trust yourself and your feelings. Be confident that things will present themselves when the time is right. Rely on yourself and trust yourself.

I can imagine that, based on these seven aiding factors, you might think; this is very vague and woolly. The aiding factors are formulated very generally. In Moneyfulness, I have given all seven factors practical handles. The main thing in the Money Method occurs between your ears, but I have very practical exercises for that. Don't be afraid and keep on reading.

Peace of Mind

Now that you survived the foundation of mindfulness, it is time to discuss the main objective of Moneyfulness. You must feel comfortable with the concept of money. It begins with the Money Method, because chances are that you first need to work on yourself, before you can proceed to the practical implementation of the Hollywood principle and Bank management.

You will only truly experience peace of mind with regard to your financial situation if you have both insight into yourself and your own behavior. Subsequently, you will address the practical organization of your money affairs. The objective is to obtain structural peace of mind without stress about money. It is fine to worry about money once in a while, because you shouldn't turn a blind eye to any dangers on the road ahead. However, as soon as you notice that it turns into structural worrying, it is time to take action. The sooner you notice the worrying behavior in yourself, the easier it is to stop doing it.

The Impact of Money

Based on a series of experiments carried out by Kathleen Vohs of the Carlson School of Management and colleagues at the University of Minnesota, I will walk you through psychological and behavioral consequences of merely the suggestion of money. A hint of money or even an unconscious perception of money makes people work harder and act more independently.

A group of people was divided in two. One group was constantly confronted with money in a subtle manner. There was a stack of monopoly money on the table, they had to read sentences with salary and wealth, there were posters on the wall with images of money and the screensaver was filled with money. In the second group, there was no single hint to or suggestion of money.

Both groups had to carry out the same tasks. The result showed that those who had been exposed to money, asked less help, but were also less eager to offer help. The same group observed a greater physical distance during conversations and spend more time alone than in the group. They were less willing to donate money than the group that hadn't seen any money-related images.

The conclusion from the study is that money is a strong motivator to do or to refrain from doing something, and money makes you more asocial.[7] Both ideas are based on the same reason. Money provides a level of independence. Even the idea of money or actually having money can make you feel more independent. Moneyfulness makes you more independent from the big bad world. The intention is by no means to teach you asocial behavior. Especially because 10% of all proceeds are used for poverty reduction. 10% of what you have paid for this book, has been added to this.

Giving

You are most likely familiar with the feeling of euphoria when you give something to others that need it. Giving affects you. The effects of giving have been studied. A number of test subjects were given a list of charities by Jorge Moll of the National institutes of health. The mere thought of being able to donate was enough to activate the brain. The reward center in the brain produces dopamine, which results on the euphoric feeling. The sense of happiness contributes to a better feeling about yourself. If you feel better about yourself, your self-confidence grows, making more stable. You are changing yourself. After you have read the Money Method, I recommend that you read this segment again. All parts of the Money Method are addressed in this. First, you change your mindset to give, then you see opportunities to contribute to society in a useful manner. You won't be stopped by your thoughts or prejudice, instead you have an objective perspective on the purpose of your money. After giving, you feel stronger and more balanced in life, which, in the end, will make you see that you are working on yourself. You have become a better person.

All elements of giving are addressed in the Money Method. This is one of the reasons to donate 10% of the proceeds to poverty reduction. The choice of poverty reduction is obvious, because you first reduce your own poverty. Whether it concerns mental poverty about money or

7   http://nymag.com/news/features/money-brain-2012-7/index3.html

an actual shortage of money is less relevant. Moneyfulness contributes to eliminate all forms of poverty as quickly as possible in the most structural way possible. Projects that require money to realize this, are just as welcome as educational projects.

ACKNOWLEDGEMENTS

In advance, I would like to apologize to anyone who has listened to my stories about the concept of Moneyfulness and who has given me feedback but who has not been individually mentioned in this acknowledgement. Hereby, I would like to thank anyone who has given their opinion in the preparation phase of the Moneyfulness process for their feedback. You have contributed to making the concept of Moneyfulness what it is today. I could have never come up with it on my own.

There are a couple of people who I would like to mention by name. For starters, my wife, Nelleke, who has had to listen to my stories about Moneyfulness again and again. I would like to thank Marriëtte Reijnders for the help and support in this book with regard to all mindfulness aspects and background. You really helped me to get on track of the true meaning of mindfulness, living the mindfulness life which I love. Juliette van Heesewijk for contributing ideas about Moneyfulness, proofreading this book and correcting my creative sentence structure. As a group, I would like to thank the pilot group. You all gave me a lot of feedback which was used to improve this book. And finally, I would like to thank

Jeff Lazarus for all he's done to get me introduced to the right people. Amongst others you introduced me to David Hancock from Morgan James Publishing and the editor Emilie Bingham.

And everyone who has been willing to hear the story of Moneyfulness.

ABOUT THE AUTHOR

Let's start with my teenage years. They were not so very successful. I was kicked out of school, had no education or relevant working experience. This continued until I reached the age of twenty-one. Then, there was someone who wanted to help me and who believed in me. I was offered to go back to school for a year. And so I did. Three years of evening schools later, I had my bachelor's degree and later on, I got my MBA at a Dutch university. But that's not the only thing; at the age of twenty-one, I was no good for anything and at the age of thirty, I was the finance director from a company that employed over 400 people and had a turnover form 40 million. All this was accomplished in nine years. When I went back to school, I realized that this was a once in a lifetime opportunity. This is what got me back on track, I've changed my mindset. I realized that my mindset was one of the most powerful things I had. This is also one of the many things that will be covered in this book.

So, I've been a finance director or business controller for about fourteen years. I had another turning point in my life, when I started my own business. I developed my online accounting software for self-employed and small business owners. I also established my own accounting and tax office. This has been changed into a franchise formula, and I have several franchisers right now.

But the start of my company didn't go smoothly. In the beginning, I ran it based on common sense. Quickly, I realized that I didn't know anything about running my own business. One of my weaknesses was to understand the human side of money, and so I attended a mindfulness training. For me as an accountant, and very analytical, attending a mindfulness training was very opposite to my personality. I discovered that the correlation between money, happiness and success is the correlation between understanding what overlaps, analytics and mindset.

Now I've combined my 25 years of experience in finance and my mindfulness expertise from the past four years into *Moneyfulness*. I'm the first one who has combined the emotional and the rational side of money. They belong together like body and soul.

You will learn to live <u>with</u> money, and you will have more money and less stress.

CPSIA information can be obtained
at www.ICGtesting.com
Printed in the USA
BVHW030923030320
573940BV00001B/150